ADMINISTRATION
SKILLS

ADMINISTRATION

SKILLS

A Practical Handbook

Edited by Debra Allcock

The Industrial Society

First published in 1994 by
The Industrial Society
Robert Hyde House
48 Bryanston Square
London W1H 7LN
Telephone: 071–262 2401

© The Industrial Society 1994

ISBN 1 85835 146 4

British Library Cataloguing-in-Publication Data.
A catalogue record for this book is available from the
British Library

Typeset by: Columns Design and Production Services Ltd, Reading
Printed by Lavenham Press
Cover design: Integra Communications, London

The Industrial Society is a registered charity. No. 290003

CONTENTS

INTRODUCTION

Many of us think of administration as paper-pushing and typing, requiring little initiative and few skills. Yet the dictionary defines an administrator as someone who manages, for example, business or public affairs, or someone capable of organising activities and resources. So why do so many organisations take their administrators for granted and ignore the skills and development needs of general administrators, secretaries and support staff?

As a result of stereotypical traditional views of administative tasks, administrators are widely undervalued and receive little recognition for their contribution to business results. Many administrators are rarely offered training and development opportunities and receive little or no career guidance. However, administrators are usually the first point of contact for internal and external customers, and they often spend a significant proportion of their time liaising with customers. They have a direct influence on their organisation's image, so an investment in training and development pays off in terms of reputation, increased custom and business access.

Administrators – for example, as managers, secretaries, personal assistants and customer service/support staff – operate at all levels across all areas of organisations. They need and use a wide range of essential skills in care areas.

It is in an organisation's interest to maximise valuable human resource by enabling employees to use their skills effectively and reach their full potential. During times of fierce labour market competition, organisations can retain experienced staff and reduce recruitment costs by addressing all employees' career development needs. It is a short-sighted economy to ignore the development needs of administrators, who comprise a significant proportion of all organisations' employees. Training them increases productivity, raises morale and helps to strengthen teams.

This *Handbook of Administration Skills* meets two important needs. Firstly, it offers administrators themselves the opportunity to review their existing skills and experience, and to learn about new skills which could improve their effectiveness in current or future jobs. Secondly, the Handbook serves as a checklist for personnel, training and other managers with responsibility for planning development programmes for administrators across their organisation. The chapters give details of the skills required of and by today's administrators, and set out guidelines on current best practice. The information is also useful for those concerned with vocational qualifications. Administrators and training managers alike will find this Handbook essential when preparing individual and organisational agendas for action on administrative development.

Jo Gardner
National Campaign Leader for Individual Development
The Industrial Society

EFFECTIVE COMMUNICATION SKILLS

Communication – what is it and how do you do it? In many different ways! Some without your even being aware of it.

Communication means interacting with others to promote understanding and achieve a result of some kind. Effectively you are trying to pass information to another person so that they can take action.

We do that through:

- Face-to-face communication
- Listening
- Questioning
- Letter writing
- Report writing
- The telephone

FACE-TO-FACE COMMUNICATION

This method of communication is often seen as the easiest. You have the person in front of you and you can explain what you mean. If the person does not understand what you are saying, you need to ask yourself:

- are you using the sort of language they understand - not technical jargon, but simple English?
- is there something about how you look that is hindering that person's understanding of what you are telling them?

It is more than just speaking to the other person.

There are three areas that matter in communication:

- words: what we say
- tone: how we say it

- body language: how we look when we are saying it

The advantages of face-to-face communication are that:

- people can '*see* what you mean'
- eye contact helps you establish if the other person is listening and understanding
- your body language can help them believe what you are saying.

Words, tone and body language also hold the key to the disadvantages of face-to-face communication.

- you can give away your true feelings
- you might 'wear your heart on your sleeve'
- the other person may not understand the words that you use
- they may not like the way you are saying the words.

Into all this can come an element over which you have no control. It may be that for some reason, which neither of you can explain, you don't like them or they don't like you!

To be an effective face-to-face communicator, you have to be aware of all the factors above. Remember it is not just words. Understanding comes from all three areas, words, tone and body language. With practice you can learn to adjust all three to match and achieve full understanding from your listener.

LISTENING SKILLS

Communication is not just one-way, with you giving all the information. You also *receive* information which involves *listening*.

Listening is more than just hearing. You often 'hear' what you want to hear. In the last section we spoke of face to face communication from the 'teller's' point of view. Listening is the other half of that communication loop and the same rules apply.

When listening, you are conscious of the other person's words, tone and body language. To these you must add your own reactions which let the communicator know you are paying attention. These reactions can include facial expressions, smiling, nodding and making comments.

When receiving information you must give the communicator your full attention, avoid making assumptions about what you *think* they are going to say and, if appropriate, make notes. This is particularly important if you are receiving information by telephone when it is easy to become distracted by what is happening around you in the office.

When listening:

- give your full attention

- do not assume what the other person is going to say

- do not waste listening time formulating what your reply will be

- show by eye contact and an interested expression that you are paying attention

- when listening on the telephone, do not allow distractions in the room to interfere with your listening abilities

- when on the phone, let your caller know you are listening by making verbal indications such as 'Mm, Yes, OK'

- make notes if appropriate, for example, when on the telephone.

QUESTIONING TECHNIQUES

When you are communicating with others there may be times when the information you have been given is not enough. If you need to know more or make clear what you are being told, you ask questions.

There are different types of questions used in different circumstances.

- Open Questions
- Closed Questions
- Specific Questions

OPEN QUESTIONS are the ones which will help you learn most.

Who? When? What? Why? Where? are the opening words to questions that will give you specific information. You cannot answer 'Yes' or 'No' to an open question.

CLOSED QUESTIONS are ones which will give you the answer 'Yes' or 'No'

'Can you?' 'Will you?' 'Did you?'

SPECIFIC QUESTIONS are ones which clarify facts. Often used for numbers, dates of birth, addresses, street numbers. They include:

'Your address is . . .?' 'Is the number . . .?'

All the techniques will enable you to understand what is being communicated to you. Remember, only by having the fullest information can you take the most appropriate action, and that is what communication is about.

EFFECTIVE USE OF THE TELEPHONE

After face to face communication the next most commonly used method is by telephone. Many aspects are

similar to face-to-face communication but the loss of observation of reactions and body language can make people less comfortable with this method.

By being more aware of how you use it (or abuse it!) at present, and thinking of how you can improve, you can become more effective on the telephone.

When speaking on the telephone you like to know that people are listening. Remember that, the next time you are receiving a call. You can let the caller know you are listening by using 'verbal nods', saying 'Yes', 'OK', 'Mm' or clarifying some of the information they are giving you.

Communicating by telephone is yet another way the profile of your organisation is perceived. For the person on the other end of the phone YOU are that organisation. If you make a bad impression, you can lose a customer forever.

There are two ways you can overcome this:

- by listening carefully and concentrating on what is being said

- by using words or your tone of voice to communicate your understanding of what is being said.

RECEIVING CALLS

Cultivate a pleasant and interesting telephone voice. It may not be your usual speaking voice but that is not important. When receiving calls, you want your caller to feel 'wanted'. Make them aware of who is speaking, what department they are dealing with. Ask the caller his/her name – we all like the sound of our own names!

When answering a call – greet your caller with

'Good morning/afternoon' and your name

Ask 'How may I help you?'

Listen carefully – make notes on a pad kept, with a pen, by the phone and only used for phone messages! Make your notes as full as possible. This will enable you to check any details with the caller before taking action.

TRANSFERRING CALLS

It may be the caller needs to be TRANSFERRED to someone else. In this case, be sure to pass on the caller's name and as many details as possible to the new person and tell the caller to whom s/he is being transferred. There can be nothing more annoying to a caller than having to tell their story over and over.

Guidelines are:

- Greet your caller, giving your name
- Offer to help
- Repeat back any message
- Say what action you will take
- DO IT!!

TAKING MESSAGES

It may be that the person your caller wants is not available. First ask them if you can help. If you can't, offer to take a message.

Messages should be kept on a pad (preferably carbonised) or message book, so that a permanent record is kept. This means that if the original message is lost, a copy is available. When telling your caller that you will take a message, you should do just that!

Say

'I will see . . . gets the message'

'I will pass the message to . . .'

NOT

'I will get him/her to phone you back'

Make the sure the message is passed on and please check that it is received. This is best done by using a message board.

MAKING CALLS

When making a call do some preparation first. Note who you are telling, their number and what your subject is. It saves your mind going blank as soon as you are connected!

You may want to consider when to make the call. Calls in the UK are cheaper after 1pm. Perhaps there is a time of day when the person you are trying to contact may be very busy and not able to speak to you.

DEVELOPING YOUR TELEPHONE SKILLS

Whether making or answering calls, there are certain skills we need to gain to make effective use of the telephone.

- preparation – by knowing as much as you can about your organisation
- controlling calls
- agreeing follow-up actions.

You can learn about your organisation by reading company materials.

Controlling calls can be achieved by using appropriate questioning techniques. Additional information can be gained from callers by using OPEN questions.

If you can learn the caller's name early in the conversation, this will also enable you to be more in control.

DIFFICULT CALLS

If you have to deal with difficult situations by telephone it is also useful to find out the person's name. People are more easily soothed if you use their name. Calls can be difficult for different reasons. It can be a technical fault, such as a bad line or that the person has been cut off. If the line is so bad that you cannot continue the call, ask the caller for their number to enable you to call them back. If the caller is cut off, apologise when they phone back.

If your caller is complaining about something, even if it is unjustified you *must* sympathise with them. Remember, you represent your organisation to them! Once you have sympathised you will find the caller usually calms down and you can then discuss the matter reasonably.

Explain what will be done about the complaint and ensure that the action is taken.

Remember, you may be the first point of contact for your organisation.

- answer calls promptly
- always use your name
- address the person by name
- control the call by appropriate questions
- only transfer a call once, if possible
- state what action you will take
- ensure you DO IT!

Effective communication will ensure your reputation and that of your organisation will be the best it can!

LETTER WRITING

It is important to have basic guidelines for writing letters. Once these are established, you can produce effective business letters, which is an important administrative skill. In order to communicate effectively you must produce quality letters for your reader.

The keys are:

- planning your letter
- writing and structuring your letter
- checking content and context.

You want to produce a letter which will be informative and interesting to the reader. It is essential that your letters are of a high standard – your reputation and that of your organisation depends upon it.

Remember that a high quality letter is an opportunity to promote your organisation.

An ideal and cheap form of advertising!

How well you present a letter can mean the difference between it being read or not!

THE STAGES OF PREPARING YOUR LETTER

PLANNING

First consider *WHY* a letter?

Is this the most appropriate form of communication?

Would a phone call do?

Could you send a fax?

Once you have decided that a letter is the form of communication you want to use, you need to identify your objective in sending the letter. For example, is it:

- to give information?
- sell an idea or an item?
- to promote an action?
- to clarify something?
- to rectify a situation?
- to promote your organisation or yourself?

Who are you writing to? How much will they already know of the subject matter of your letter? What is their status in the company? The more you know about your reader, the easier it will be to write a letter to which they will respond.

Once you have done all this you can then start to think about the content to your letter. Check all your facts and details and then make notes of all you want to say. You may decide to jot these down in a column.

This could be an opportunity to try out a 'Pattern Note'. On a plain sheet write your subject in the centre and from it draw lines to each idea you have. From this basis you can decide the best order of your letter.

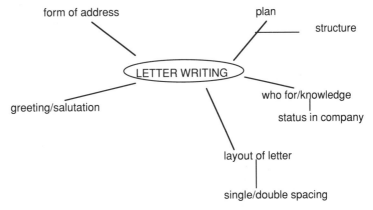

Pattern note drawn to show example

Write the subject of your letter in the centre and from that point 'brainstorm', letting your thoughts run. Join your thoughts to the centre theme with straight lines. Allow your thoughts to flow freely, anything you don't finally need can be discarded later by circling unwanted items in your note.

Prioritise your items by numbering them. Group ideas together.

Now you have all your thoughts on paper you can go on to the next step.

STRUCTURE OF LETTER

You do not want your letter to be too long – one page in length should be sufficient. Likewise, be aware of the length of sentences and paragraphs. Modern language that is understandable is easier to read then jargon with which the reader may be unfamiliar.

- letter length should be only one page
- try to keep sentence length to not more than 20 words
- paragraph length should be no more than four sentences.

Structure your letter around the following:

- Greeting
- Heading
- Introduction
- Information
- Action
- Conclusion

GREETING

'Dear Sir/Madam' is used if you do not know the name of the person to whom you are writing.

'Dear Dr/Mr/Mrs/Ms/Miss' is professional and less formal. Ms is quite correct if you have no indication of marital status.

'Dear Mary or Brian' – if you know the person or if this form of greeting is appropriate in your line of business.

If you are in doubt, phone the organisation to check. There is nothing more off-putting than receiving a letter with your name wrongly spelled.

HEADING

A heading after the greeting immediately tells the reader the subject of the letter. Use a heading that means something to the reader. Eg don't use *'Re Order Number 74021'* — Use *'Your order for a laser printer'*.

INTRODUCTION

In the first introductory paragraph, say why you are writing and mention the date of any correspondence received from them.

> 'Thank you for your letter of 10th June 1993'.

> 'As requested in your letter of 20th June 1993, I enclose our price-list'.

INFORMATION

This is the main part of the letter when you deal with the subject referred to in your heading. From your notes you will be able to decide on the order of the information. Use paragraphs and if necessary use sub-headings for each new subject.

> *'Payment* – our terms are 30 days net.'

> *'Methods of payment* – cheques payable to . . .'

> *'Overdue accounts* – interest on overdue accounts will be charged at 1% per week.'

ACTION

Your letter should say

- what action is required

- when it needs to be actioned by (give deadlines)
- who should take the action

Actions should be achievable.

CONCLUSION

This paragraph enables you to personalise your letter.

'I look forward to hearing from you'.

'Thank you for your help over the last month'

This is less formal and old fashioned than

'Please do not hesitate to contact me'

'Our best attention is assured at all times'

WRITING THE LETTER

Writing your letter should be as easy as ABC

- accurate
- brief
- clear.

You are not out to impress your reader with your flowery style of writing. You are creating a letter which s/he will want to read and contains information which is easily understood.

ACCURATE

- check that your facts are accurate

- make sure names are correctly spelled

- use words accurately and appropriately.

BRIEF

Be brief – keep it short. Your reader's time is as precious as yours. You don't want to spend hours writing a letter – s/he doesn't want to spend hours reading one.

Short sentences are easier to understand.

- 4% of readers understand a 27 word sentence first time

- 75% of readers understand a 17 word sentence first time

- 95% of readers understand an 8 word sentence first time.

Try to keep sentences to less than 20 words.

Use short words and phrases. The effect is greater.

Long Word	Short Word
Proceed	Go ahead
Terminate	End
Purchase	Buy

Can you think of others?

Phrase	Short version
At this moment in time	Now
In the event of	If
We have pleasure in enclosing	We enclose

Your letter will be clearer if you have:

- used a heading

- paragraphed your information in a logical sequence

● used simple language – not jargon.

The tone of your letter is important. Obviously there may be times when you have to write a letter of apology. It should, however, be possible to use a positive tone in all your letters, even letters of apology, eg.

> 'I am sorry you were unhappy with the accommodation provided. May I invite you to have dinner here with our compliments'.

Be aware of how you phrase your sentences. Try to avoid sounding too formal. Letters today are professional AND friendly. Over-formality is considered stuffy and impresses very few.

PUNCTUATION

In the modern business letter, there is less punctuation now than 20 years ago. Then addresses, greetings and endings all had commas and full stops. Now, you only need punctuation in the actual body of the letter. Commas are used to separate nouns in a sentence such as:

> 'We will check all fire exits, extinguishers and safety equipment'.

Semi colons are not widely used in the modern letter. It is better to start a new sentence.

A *colon* is used when listing information.

> 'The price includes:
> All paper
> All paint and emulsion
> Paste
> Labour charges'

The *apostrophe* indicates ownership or is used when a

letter is omitted.

> John's car
> The men's room

> 'We don't want that!' – rather than – 'We do not want that!'

LAYOUT

Your company may have a 'house style' which you can check from your files. Perhaps there is flexibility of style which would allow you to suggest different layouts for different types of letters.

CHECKING

Checking letters for accuracy before presentation for signature is important for the administrator. Managers should also be encouraged to check – but not to use this as an excuse to make changes!

Check:

- layout – does it look attractive, evenly spaced?
- punctuation and spelling – are they accurate?
- names/titles/addresses – all correct?

Do not just use a Spell Check system to gauge accuracy. This will not pick up on words which are correctly spelled but wrongly placed.

Read the letter aloud or get someone else to read it out to you while you check your own copy.

It can be difficult to see errors in letters you have typed yourself.

Make sure you have the correct number of copies.

REPORT WRITING

Like letter writing, the first thing you need to think of when asked to write a report is:

- Who is my reader?

- What does s/he already know of this subject?

- What are the objectives of this report (do I want to sell, persuade etc.)?

You may also want to consider why you have been asked to write the report

- are you an expert in this subject?

- are you the best report writer in the organisation?

- have you been asked 'because you were there?'

PLANNING THE REPORT

- consider how long it is until the report is required.

- how long do you have to work on gathering the information?

- how long on structuring and writing the report?

- how long on checking, revising and perhaps even retyping the report?

Once you have established the answers to these questions you can then begin to prepare.

Will your reader be technical or non-technical? This will be important in the decision of how you will phrase your final submission.

As with letter writing you will wish to make notes on

your subject. Use a plain sheet and try a pattern note (see page 11 for information about pattern notes). Now you have all your thoughts on paper you can go on to the next step.

RESEARCH

If your subject is complicated and will require a lot of research you can transfer your topics to a further page and put it into columns.

Topics to investigate	Sources	Information Required	Action
What I need to know	Where to find it	Additional Information	Overheads

Using these notes you can build up a file of information about the topics to be discussed/presented in your report. Once complete you can decide the order of presentation.

STRUCTURE

The following structure is suggested:

- title page
- contents
- summary
- introduction
- findings
- conclusion
- recommendation

- appendices, acknowledgements, references, bibliography
- Index.

THE TITLE PAGE

Should include:

- the title
- the author's name
- who the report is prepared for
- date prepared
- reference number, if appropriate.

CONTENTS

Listed in sequence and numbered with references.

SUMMARY

A brief outline of the report, including the recommendations.

INTRODUCTION

This tells the reader about the report and should include:

- who authorised the report
- who carried out the investigation

- the purpose of the report
- name the sources of information
- a brief background into the subject matter of the report.

FINDINGS (OR MAIN TEXT)

This is the section of the report which presents your information. From your earlier prepared notes, detail your information in language which will be understood by your reader. Paragraph each topic with a sub-heading to make it more interesting and easier to read. Number the separate sub-paragraphs appropriately.

CONCLUSIONS

This is where you draw together all the findings, and, as the title suggests, 'come to a conclusion'. You will want to express that these conclusions are your own from the investigation which proceeded the report.

RECOMMENDATIONS

This section offers the reader your solution to the problem. Based on the findings of your report and the conclusion reached, the recommendations are actions which you think should now be taken. These should also be written in jargon-free terms.

Recommendations may be single, or several. List your recommendations. Should action need to be taken by individuals, name them and give a date by when action should be taken and reported back.

As with letter writing, the tone of your language is all important! You are recommending – trying to win either their approval or support – be kind.

> 'Following on the conclusions that . . . I can now recommend . . .'

APPENDICES

This can include:

- a glossary of technical terms used in the report

- a list of abbreviations

- a back-up reading list

- additional items relevant to the report

- acknowledgements – thanking contributors to the report

- references – additional material used which is normally unavailable

- bibliography – readily available sources of information used – books etc.

INDEX

Can be used when the report is very large.

As was noted for letter writing, the following is important

Accuracy

Brevity

Clarity

Be willing to take ownership of the report you have written and use language which will be meaningful to the reader.

PRESENTATION/TYPING

Decide on the layout you want – presentation is everything!

The actual layout should encourage the reader to go on reading. Wide margins, double spacing and paragraphs with headings will enhance the appearance of your hard work.

Type the headings in a difference type-face or in emboldened type to make the subject stand out.

Be consistent in your numbering system.

- alphabetical
- decimal
- Roman numerical

Use whatever will help your reader best.

TAKING A BREAK

Once your report is in draft form it can help to take break from it. Leave your work for 24 hours before reviewing it with fresh eyes. It may be that once you see it in typed form you will want to revise part of it.

Be sure to brief your typist. If you are new to report writing, ask their advice about layout – they may be able to show you examples of different reports they have typed in the past.

REVISING YOUR WORK

Read your typed draft from start to finish. Mark any areas to be changed but do not start work on them yet. Once you have completed the read-through try to look at it from the reader's point of view.

- how does it appear now that it is 'in print'?
- is the information in a logical order?
- is the language understandable?
- are the conclusions and recommendations convincing?
- will your report achieve its objectives?

Deal with any changes required in the body of the text.

Return to the beginning and review each page, checking accuracy of facts, figures, names, dates.

Check each section, starting with the Title Page and ensure all necessary information is in place and in the correct order.

Only when this is complete can a final typewritten copy be made.

THE SUMMARY

This document is a brief version of your report. Its inclusion will ensure that even the busiest reader of your report will know its contents.

Its purpose is to:

- introduce the report
- indicate to the reader the contents
- give a quick overview to the busy reader.

To create a summary:

- read the whole report
- decide on the main theme
- reduce detail to statements
- include conclusions and recommendations.

Good luck!

SUMMARY

- choose the most appropriate form of communication to get your message across
- in all communication be accurate, brief and clear
- be aware of your body language and tone of voice when communicating face-to-face or on the telephone
- LISTEN
- use open questions
- Prepare for all letters and reports.

AN INTRODUCTION TO ASSERTIVENESS

The concept of assertiveness first became popular in Britain in the 1970's and was associated with the upsurge in The Women's Campaign. The common misconception was that, by learning to be assertive, you would metamorphose into an uncaring, selfish person with impressive shoulder pads! 'If you are going to be trained to be assertive, I'm taking lessons in self defence!' said a manager to a secretary!

Living in a world that is overshadowed by competition and comparison it can be difficult to understand that assertiveness is not about winning, but *is* about self esteem and respect for others.

It is now largely recognised that assertive behaviour provides both men and women with the skills that enable them to communicate successfully at work. It is a life skill and one that is constantly refined and developed as you grow in confidence. It is not a gimmick or trick, but a skill that can be learnt step by step. Assertiveness is about modifying behaviour – not changing personalities. It encourages you to think about the choices you make in the way you behave, and the results you get. Assertiveness is the key to good, clear, honest, professional communication. As administrators you provide the first line of communication for your organisation – both internally and externally. Therefore, it is critical that you are able to deal with situations effectively. What do you say and feel if:

- your manager makes an unreasonable request of you?

- you want to disagree with the point of view of a senior member of staff?

- you get an angry customer on the telephone who is shouting abuse?

By developing an assertive approach you will be in a more confident position to:

- avoid conflict situations

- save time (and money)

- get more of what you want

- handle your appraisal

- work more effectively with your manager and colleagues

- put forward your ideas and thoughts

- feel good about yourself and your behaviour.

This chapter does not come with a magic wand! However, if you follow the advice set out it will provide the building blocks for you to become more assertive at work and home.

UNDERSTANDING BEHAVIOUR

The outcome of any situation is dependent on the way you choose to behave. The old saying 'Behaviour breeds behaviour' is very true. Whether you are initiating some action or responding to someone else's behaviour you will have three options to choose:

(a) Passive (non–assertive, submissive)

(b) Aggressive (direct, indirect)

(c) Assertive

PASSIVE

You are passive when you avoid making a stand in order to maintain the status quo, allow others to make decisions for you, verbally agree with others despite your real feelings, procrastinate to avoid problem solving

What would you look like?

- standing back (sit at the back of groups)
- little or no eye contact
- smiling even when upset
- fidgeting

What would you sound like?

- apologetic
- vague
- self hating
- hesitant
- moaning

How would you feel?

- taken advantage of
- hurt
- anxious
- frustrated
- powerless

How would the other feel?

- frustrated
- resentful
- exasperated
- guilty

So, passive behaviour doesn't help you to achieve your goals therefore, you feel a victim and blame others for what happens to you. By being passive you allow others to choose for you. You will often choose passive behaviour because it is low risk, we become invisible and can opt out.

AGGRESSIVE

You are aggressive when you try to impose your position on others; always make decisions for others; accuse, blame and find fault with others despite their feelings; act with belligerence and humiliate others; behave in an unpredictable and explosive manner.

What would you look like?

- leaning forward
- pointing fingers
- piercing or glaring eye contact
- jabbing

What would you sound like?

- loud
- sarcastic
- emphatic
- defensive
- arrogant

How would you feel?

- in control of others
- guilty
- isolated
- power over them

How would others feel?

- defensive

- humiliated

- afraid

- resentful

So, aggressive behaviour does help you to achieve our goals to a limited extent. However this is gained at the expense of others. If you frequently behave aggressively, people will stop co-operating as they will resent having decisions made for them. Aggressive behaviour is 'high risk' as it sets you up in a very visible way.

ASSERTIVE

Y ou are assertive when you are honest with yourself and others; protect your own rights, but respect the rights of others; are able to express yourself socially and emotionally; have confidence in yourself and are able to behave in an adult, rational way.

What would you look like?

- eye control is direct, but not staring

- relaxed, moving easily

- open hand movements

- head held up

How would you sound?

- steady and firm

- spontaneous

- sincere

- clear

How would we feel?

- good about self

- confident

- responsible for our actions

- power within

So, assertive behaviour helps us to achieve our goals, without hurting others. It is about choosing for ourselves and taking responsibility for our own actions. It can provide us with a gentle, focused strength and inner confidence.

Behaviour

Attitude
Feelings
Beliefs
Perception

In any situation, the way in which you behave is what others will see and respond to. However, what you may not always be aware of is the other person's feelings, beliefs, etc., that underpin that behaviour . . . which is just the tip of the iceburg. It might be that you have had a terrible morning. . . you got toothpaste down your shirt; the car wouldn't start, you missed the bus and the first thing your manager says to you is 'you're late!'. . . All s/he sees is the aggression as you snap 'I know, I do have a watch!'.

In order to practice assertive behaviour you must ensure positive, assertive beliefs, feelings and attitudes.

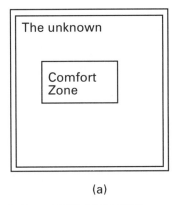 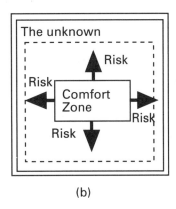

(a) (b)

COMFORT ZONES

There is always an element of risk when you try something new. In order to grow you must come out of your 'comfort zone' and take risks.

(a) The comfort zone represents those situations you enjoy, are practised at and are good at i.e. things you feel comfortable doing.

The unknown represents those situations you find un pleasant and difficult. You will do everything in your power to avoid them!
    You remain static.

(b) The dotted box represents your potential. If you come outside your comfort zone and take a small risk, you will increase the size of your comfort zone. By regularly taking risks you will always grow.

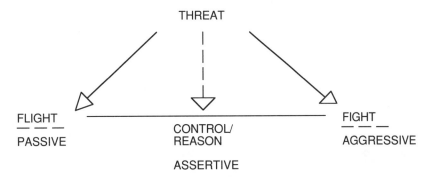

Areas outside comfort zones provide a threat. You will usually respond by returning to your 'flight or fight' syndrome – either back off or lash out. Look for the middle ground of reasoned control that handles the threat situation in a careful and adult way.

SELF-ESTEEM AND CONFIDENCE

In order to be able to behave assertively you need to build a clear idea of your own opinion. Our culture does not encourage us to evaluate ourselves and we expect our parents, teachers, colleagues, friends to tell us how we are doing. If they criticise us we sulk and get upset, or justify ourselves; and it they praise, we are pleased. It is important that you can, and do, evaluate your own behaviour.

To start with, confidence is just that . . . a con! You smile on the outside when really your knees are knocking and your stomach is in knots. As you develop your self-esteem you will also notice an inner strength developing.

EXERCISE:

1 Take a sheet of paper and list all the things you are good at
2 Take a separate sheet of paper and list all those things you could improve on
   Which is the longer list?!
3 Now, convert list 2 into positives.

Carry out this exercise on a regular basis. By identifying what you are good at you can remind yourself of your strengths and build your self esteem.

INNER DIALOGUE

How often does the 'chatterbox' in your head affect your behaviour?

e.g.　　Thoughts on the way to your annual appraisal

　　　　. . . 'I don't think my boss likes me'

　　　　. . . 'I'm bound to say the wrong thing'

　　　　. . . 'I wish I hadn't asked for time off to go to college'

　　　　. . . 'I haven't met all my targets'

By the time you start the appraisal you look anxious, you're biting your bottom lip and you are staring into space

SITUATION → INNER VOICE → FEELINGS/THOUGHTS → BEHAVIOUR

What if you had harnessed the strength of that 'chatterbox' to influence your behaviour?

　　　　. . . 'I feel good about this'

　　　　. . . 'I made a good job of re-organising the office systems'

　　　　. . . 'I've worked hard this year'

　　　　. . . 'I've taken on extra responsibility'

　　　　. . . 'I can tell her about my college course'

Now when you start the appraisal you are relaxed, smiling and open about your thoughts

SITUATION → POSITIVE INNER VOICE → POSITIVE FEELINGS/THOUGHTS → ASSERTIVE BEHAVIOUR

In order to behave assertively, you must think and believe assertively

> * I am responsible for what happens to me
>
> * I can choose how I behave in a situation

So, to be assertive you *must* first consider your behaviour and your beliefs. *Then*, you can think about how.

THE FIRST STEPS TO ASSERTIVENESS

Like any other skill, assertiveness can be learnt – much the same as learning to ride a bike. It will seem strange and cumbersome at first; but with practice it will become easier and more natural.

By identifying the key stages in the communication process you will be able to handle situations assertively. You are already using many of the skills with success. All you need is a framework to enable you to understand why a certain response worked, and to ensure that you are able to respond with the same confidence in the future.

It is very important that you *RESPOND* to situations. Many of us plunge straight in with a reaction and end up

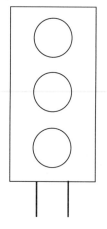

STOP: Assess the situation. Consider your inner dialogue, your body language.

LOOK: Observe the other person. What are they telling you through their posture and expression?

&

LISTEN: Listen to the message - the words. Do you understand?

RESPOND ASSERTIVELY

coming away thinking 'that wasn't what I wanted to say,' 'I should have said,' 'that was awful'.

To help us respond to a situation we should STOP, LOOK AND LISTEN.

THE FIRST THREE STEPPING STONES

By taking the following three steps you have taken in the other person's point of view, their needs and feelings; with this in mind you have stated your side of things clearly and honestly, and have described what you would like to happen.

The 3 steps should follow closely together. Don't hang around, or pad out the statements. Often you will carry out steps 1 & 2 and then fail to say what it is *you want*. It is only by following through with step 3 that you are giving yourselves the chance of 'getting what you want'. 'If you don't ask, you won't get!'

EXAMPLE:

You are busy and under pressure. A colleague comes up to your desk and begins to pour out her troubles.

Assertive Response:	'Wendy, you seem to have a lot on your mind at the moment, however, I'm in the middle of meeting a tight deadline and I'm not able to chat now. I'd like to catch up with you at lunch time.'
Step 1:	You have understood that Wendy is troubled and wants to chat.
Step 2:	You have said that now is not a good time for you.
Step 3:	You have explained that you would like to meet her later.

EXAMPLE:

You are at a team meeting. You begin to make what you believe to be a useful suggestion for loaning out files to prevent them going missing. You are cut short by one of the managers who comments that all these petty admin details take up so much time there's none left for doing the real job.

Assertive Response: 'Sarah, I know that admin details do take up quite a bit of time during these meetings. However, I feel that good procedures are vital for the smooth running of the office and I would like to finish discussing the filing system now.'

Step 1: You have understood that admin takes time during the meeting.

Step 2: You have said how you feel — that admin procedures are important.

Step 3: You have stated what you want to happen — to finish discussing the filing now.

THE FIRST THREE STEPPING STONES

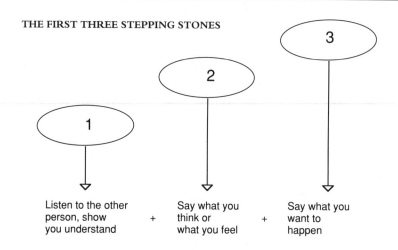

Listen to the other person, show you understand   +   Say what you think or what you feel   +   Say what you want to happen

EMPATHY

Step 1 is very important. It enables you to recognise that the other person has feelings too. If you plunge straight in with 'I think, I want' you could be seen as being aggressive.

Empathy shows that you are not dismissing the other person or their situation, but are still able to assert your position too. It is not to be confused with sympathy. If you are sympathetic you feel sorry for the other person. Empathy is important in conflict situations.

ASSERTIVE BODY LANGUAGE

Earlier in the chapter we talked about the three behaviour types and looked at how body language reinforces that behaviour. You need to ensure that when you are responding to a situation assertively you choose assertive body language to help support the message. It is important that your body doesn't give a contradictory message — it must work for you, not against you.

When going into a situation think about:

- Where are you in relation to the other person?

  - are you too close, too far away?

  - sitting down, whilst they stand?

- What is your facial expression?

  - is it appropriate?

  - are you looking at the other person?

- What is the rest of your body doing?

  - are you upright?

  - are you fiddling with your jacket button?

EXERCISE:

Get a good friend or colleague to observe your body language for a few days. Ask for honest, constructive feedback.

Often, you do not know how you look. Why is it that you always gasp when you see yourself on your friend's wedding video?

WHAT WORDS SHOULD YOU USE?

The key to assertive language is 'ownership'. Assertiveness is about speaking up for what you think or feel therefore:

- Use 'I' statements
    'I think . . .'
    'I want . . .'
    'My idea . . .'

- Use factual descriptions, not judgements
    'Your typing is useless!' (Aggressive)
    'Your typing often needs correcting' (Assertive)

- Express thoughts and feelings
    'I feel angry about . . .'
    'I was upset when you . . .'

- Use clear statements – don't waffle
    'I know you're very busy, and you probably have a thousand other more important things to do, I wouldn't ask but I'm desperate, would you mind doing some photocopying for me' (Passive)
    'Will you please do some photocopying for me?' (Assertive request)

GETTING TO WIN/WIN

There will be occasions when you practice the three first steps to assertiveness, clearly state what it is you want to happen, and the other person will agree with you. Great! In those situations you will find yourselves getting more of what you want.

However often, you will state your position assertively and the other person will want more information, argue or disagree. In these situations, you must ensure that both parties come away from the situation in a positive position – look for a win/win solution.

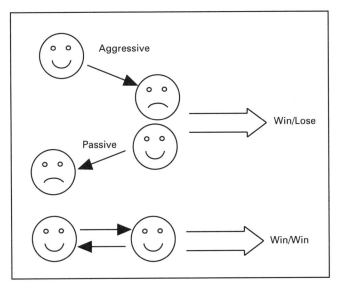

Negotiate a joint solution which is acceptable to all – a *workable compromise*. The negotiation should give each person room to manoeuvre in order to work out a solution that is satisfactory for all.

> YOUR solution + MY solution = OUR SOLUTION

EXAMPLE:

Your manager wants you to stay late and finish a report. You are going out tonight and do not want to stay late.

You: 'Mike, I know this report is needed tomorrow afternoon, however, I can't stay late this evening so I suggest you ask someone else this time'
(3 basic steps)

Mike: 'But I've asked everyone, you're my last hope, go on – please?!'

You: 'I can't work late this evening, however, as it is important I'm prepared to come in early tomorrow.'

(Suggesting workable compromise)

Mike: 'I really wanted to proof it this evening, but we could squeeze it in in the morning.'

You: 'OK then leave it on my desk and I'll do it first thing tomorrow.'

Remember, your goal is self respect – not necessarily getting your own way.

Although neither Mike or you are 100% happy with the solution, it is at least one that you can both live with and *you* have stood up for yourself by not staying late.

N.B.

Not all situations will be negotiable. If you have very strong views you may not want to compromise. However, for communications at work to be effective there has to be give and take. If you never negotiate you will be seen as always wanting your own way.

FURTHER ASSERTIVE TECHNIQUES

So far we have considered the first steps of the skill of assertiveness:

1 Listen to the other person, show you understand

2 Say what you think or feel

3 Say what you want to happen

   If there is disagreement . . .

4 Look for a workable compromise

As you practice those steps you may well find that they have limitations – 'What if the other person isn't listening to me?', 'First they said they wanted to help, now they're saying they can't'. However there are additional techniques to the basic model in order to help deal with these situations.

BROKEN RECORD

Broken record is the skill of calmly repeating what you want, over and over again – just like a stuck record! It should be used when someone is ignoring, or not hearing your message. It is saying – 'Until we discuss and resolve this issue, we are not moving on'. It is a very strong technique and over use could constitute aggressive behaviour. The tone of voice is calm and polite.

FOGGING

'Fogging' helps deal with unconstructive criticism. Unconstructive criticism is often the result of anger felt by the other person being dumped on you! You can defuse the situation by acknowledging the criticism without agreeing with it. This makes the other person slow down – just like driving into a 'fog bank'. Because they have nothing solid to go on and they meet no resistance, there is nothing to fuel their anger. This gives you both time to get things on a more even keel.

NEGATIVE FEELINGS ASSERTION

Negative feelings assertion is the skill of revealing negative feelings that you are experiencing as a result of a situation – 'I am upset' 'I am angry'. This does not mean becoming blaming or judgmental in any way. It does mean stating your case clearly and constructively about what is happening, how you feel about it and what you would like to happen.

DISCREPANCY ASSERTION

Discrepancy assertion is the skill of pointing out to someone the inconsistency in their behaviour, without blame or accusation. This helps to clear misunderstandings before they grow into difficult issues. With discrepancy assertion it is important to be as objective as possible pointing out known facts clearly and leaving the door open for discussion and resolution. It will often help you move towards a workable compromise.

SUMMARY AND ACTION

Learning to be assertive takes time – the same as learning any other new skill. By reading this chapter you won't suddenly be a more assertive person. To be able to respond assertively to situations at work you will need to practice and practice, and practice! It is important you get the basics right first – start with situations you feel comfortable with and move onto those nightmare scenarios later! Have a go, and learn from your mistakes.

You must remember that assertiveness has its limitations – it isn't always appropriate behaviour and you will need to make choices. It's not an obligation. You can choose not to be assertive and that is OK too, providing you take responsibility for the consequences. And don't forget, everyone's self-esteem has its off days!

By choosing to behave more assertively you will:

- develop a sense of self worth

- be more relaxed and open

- be less critical of yourself (and others)

- know what you want from a situation

- develop the skills to handle difficult situations.

'People travel to wonder at the height of mountains; at the huge waves of the sea; at the long courses of rivers; at the vast compass of the ocean; at the circular motion of the stars; and they pass themselves by without wondering'

St Augustine

So, what steps can you take to be more assertive? Try moving up the building blocks step by step until assertiveness becomes a way of life!

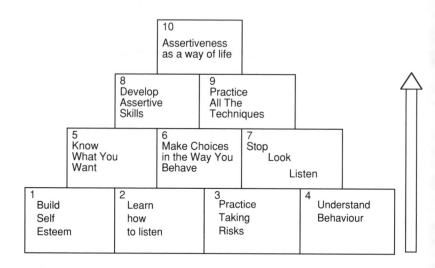

FURTHER READING

A Woman in Your Own Right, Anne Dickson – Quartet
I'm OK, You're OK, Tom Harris – Pan Books
A Guide to Assertiveness, Paddy O'Brien – The Industrial
   Society Press
Assertiveness at Work, Ken & Kate Bake – McGraw-Hill

3 CUSTOMER CARE

WHAT IS CUSTOMER CARE?

THE CUSTOMER

When you are at work you do not work in isolation. You depend on others, your colleagues, your team, your manager, other departments and of course ultimately the customer. The customer is the person who buys your products or services (commercial organisations) or uses or depends on your services (i.e. public sector, voluntary organisations). You are dealing with people all the time. All these people have needs and wants, expectations and desires. All are different. For the purposes of this chapter, whoever you deal with at work whether it be an 'internal' or and 'external' person will be called a *customer*. We *all* have *customers*.

- A customer is *ANYONE* you deal with at work who *RECEIVES* a product or service *FROM* you.

THE SUPPLIER

In the paragraph above you are the supplier of a product or service. You become a customer when you receive a product or service from someone else.

- A supplier is *ANYONE* you deal with at work who *PROVIDES* a product or service *FOR* you.

A DEFINITION OF CUSTOMER CARE

There are many definitions.
One is:

'Customer Care is a COMPLEX series of relationships between customers and suppliers. It is to do with the NATURE of the relationships and the MANAGEMENT OF THE INTERACTION between them'.

- ● COMPLEX — dealing with people is very complex
- ● NATURE — the behavioural aspects, i.e. body language, language, tone, mood
- ● MANAGEMENT OF INTERACTION — the systems and procedures in all organisations to maintain standards, quality and consistency.

A successful outcome means a satisfied customer. To achieve this, three things need to be considered in any organisation — Strategy, Systems and Staff and they all need to be focused on the Customer. see Fig.1.

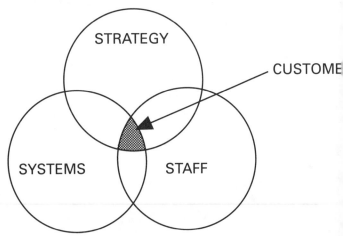

Figure 1

You can have wonderful staff who deal with customers really well. They agree things with the customers only to find that the system behind them fails.

You can have wonderful systems that consistently deliver quality products and services only to have poorly trained staff dealing with the customer on the front line.

You can have the staff and systems working well, only to discover the organisation has no idea where it's going or no way of keeping in touch with what its customers really want. All three areas must be considered by organisations, always remembering that the customer is the focal point.

MOMENTS OF TRUTH

Whenever you start to deal with a customer you can consider it to be a Moment Of Truth (MOT). An MOT can occur 3 ways:

(a) Face-to-face

(b) On the telephone

(c) When you receive or send written communication

Let's consider what you're representing at a face-to-face MOT:

- with external customers – your organisation

- with internal customers – your department

- with anyone – yourself!

Whatever your role within an organisation, you play a very important part in creating the 'image' for your organisation or department.

e.g.   I was talking recently to someone who had just returned from Greece. They were saying how friendly the Greek people were. Yet how many Greeks had they met? Not many, yet those few had influenced the perception of the holiday maker who now thought all Greeks were friendly! It can be the same with your organisation, where you can and do influence people's perception of it. e.g. How many times have you said 'Oh, I've got to go to so and so department!' (Sigh, sigh!). It's not the 'department' that's the problem it's the people in it!

To create good impressions it helps if you feel good about yourself and what you are doing. If you don't you should ask yourself why and try to do something about it. Don't be afraid to ask for help or confide in a close friend. **Remember, you don't get a second chance to make a first impression!**

THE FIRST LAW OF SERVICE

This states that SATISFACTION EQUALS EXPECTATIONS MINUS PERCEPTIONS
   Lets consider the elements.

(a) EXPECTATIONS: Everyone has expectations when approaching a situation. Going to see a film or play – you may be expecting to laugh, be frightened, be excited, be sad.

  • Going to work – overcrowding, cancellations, stress.

  • Going to the dentist – fear, pain, needles!

How are these expectations formulated? By past experiences, recommendations, media, upbringing, school etc. Try to imagine what the customer is expecting from you and your organisation. The best way to do this is to put yourself in their shoes. What would you expect. Make a list. Keep it with you. There is a pretty good chance that if you fulfil the expectations you have for yourself, then your customer will be satisfied too. See Appendix 1 for a list of expectations.

(b) PERCEPTION: As the customer is dealt with by you they collect information about you and your organisation. They also experience emotions and pick up the 'vibes'. From this information, they form an opinion of the 'experience' with you and then compare this with their expectations. Broadly, three things can then happen.

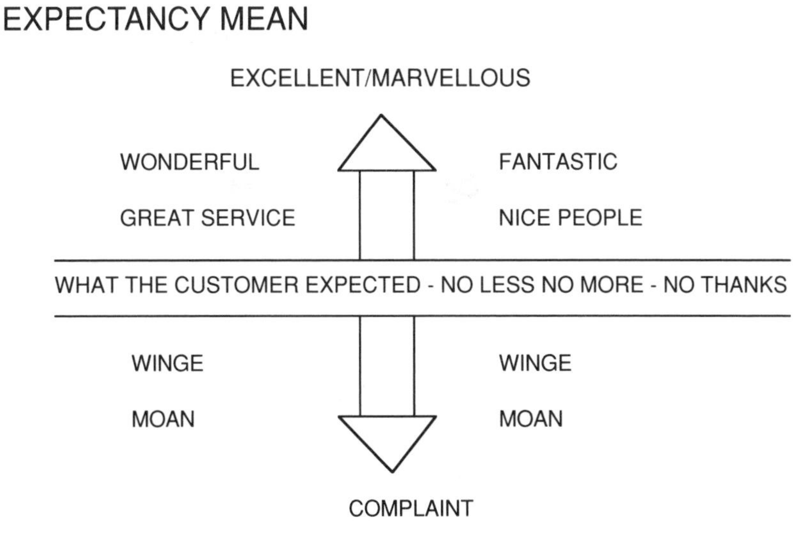

EXPECTANCY MEAN

EXCELLENT/MARVELLOUS

WONDERFUL   FANTASTIC

GREAT SERVICE   NICE PEOPLE

WHAT THE CUSTOMER EXPECTED - NO LESS NO MORE - NO THANKS

WINGE   WINGE

MOAN   MOAN

COMPLAINT

Figure 2

They may consider the experience to be average. The service providers were O.K. There was no hassle. The product or service was easy to find or obtain. Not a particularly memorable experience at all. The majority of moments of truth are like this.

Things change when their perception is out of line with their expectations. E.g. You book a table for 8 p.m. at a restaurant for a special occasion. You arrive on time only to be told that your table isn't ready and that it will be about 10 minutes. Your expectations are now set at 10 minutes. You expect to be at your table within that time. 10 minutes go by, 15 minutes, 20 minutes! There has been no explanation from the restaurant staff and you are fuming with anger. However good the service and meal is after this the damage has been done. You probably won't use that restaurant ever again and you will certainly tell other people about your bad experience. Research has shown that we tell between 7–15 people about our bad experiences. If the customers feel we have not fulfilled their expectations they will winge, moan and possibly complain.

What we want all our customers to be feeling and saying 'great service, nice people etc'. But how do you do it? There are three simple stages.

1 You find out what the customer wants, needs and is expecting by careful questioning and observation.

2 You fulfil those needs, wants and expectations to the best of your ability and within the scope of your responsibility and authority.

3 Then you do a *little bit extra*. It can be the smallest thing, just to tip the balance from average to very good. A smile, use of the customer name, an extra piece of information or advice.

Your customer will then go away thinking, 'yes, that was a good experience, I enjoyed it!'

KEY POINTS

- find out what the customerwants/needs/expects
- satisfy them if possible and then do something extra.

CUSTOMER CARE STANDARDS

Having some basic customer care standards can be very useful, both for employees and the organisation. Employees know what's expected and the organisation can measure performance objectively. It is important to distinguish the tangible and intangible areas i.e. the systems and procedural standards and the personal, behavioural standards.

TANGIBLE

Tangible standards are usually broken down into action. For example:

- speed of response to customer queries eg – answer telephone within three rings

- type of response eg answer with – 'Good morning/afternoon, Personnel Department, Joanne speaking'

- format of written response eg standard letters, use printed message pads etc

- customer complaints – eg clear procedures about who's responsible, how to follow up etc

- environmental/image – signing in when arriving at a building, clear layout of reception, organisation of space, health & safety, staff dress/uniforms, use of the customer's name etc.

INTANGIBLE

Intangible standards are more difficult to set and monitor. By their nature they are more subjective and are influenced by individual managers who decide whether a particular behaviour is acceptable or not. But they can and should be set.

eg   Smile at each moment of truth

         Make eye contact

         Use a pleasant tone of voice

One way of setting standards is to use an objective support grid. See Appendix 2. List the names of the individuals/departments you deal with frequently at work along the top of the grid and down the left hand side. Take each name and working down and across, where the columns meet is that persons square into which they enter the key tasks of their job the other squares are used to enter whatever support the others can give the individual to enable them to effectively carry out these tasks. The type of support usually works out to be types of information, accuracy or meeting deadlines. All the parties concerned repeat the process for each other ending up with a completed grid containing clear work instructions and standards of performance:

KEY POINTS

- discuss agree and set measurable standards of performance
- monitor these regularly
- strive to continually improve standards.

HANDLING COMPLAINTS

Even with the best will in the world things go wrong and

customers get upset. How complaints are handled is a very important aspect of customer care. You can lose a customer forever if they are handled poorly, but gain a really loyal customer if they are handled well. Why do people shop at M&S? Because there's no problem if there's a problem! There are some key steps to successful complaint handling:

- ensure responsibilities and authorities are clear

- ensure the person in the front line knows how to deal with complaints or who to refer them to

- ensure the customer is allowed to fully explain in their own words what the problem is. DO NOT INTERRUPT, GO ON THE DEFENSIVE OR BE RUDE OR ANGRY BACK. LISTEN, MAKE NOTES

- when the customer has 'had their say', APOLOGISE and then confirm that you have all the details and ask questions for clarification

- get the customer's details, name address etc

- take positive action. Explain what can be done and how long it will take – confirm that this is acceptable to the customer

- take the agreed action or refer it to someone who can

- within a specified time, check that the complaint has been resolved satisfactorily

- thank the customer for raising the point

- if possible take action to avoid a similar thing happening to another customer in the future

DO

- listen
- make notes
- apologise
- confirm details
- take action
- use the customer's name
- follow up
- stay calm
- be polite and positive

DON'T

- interrupt
- transfer too soon

- be rude
- get angry
- be sarcastic or dissuasive
- pass the buck
- take it personally

Some customers can be very demanding and difficult. It is wise to take a few minutes to recover before attempting another moment of truth, if this is at all possible. If not, consider rotating the people who take initial calls or deal first with customers face-to-face. If the customer becomes really abusive or personal, then always refer him/her to a more senior person.

SUMMARY POINTS

- be aware of the importance of your role in Customer Care
- everybody has customers both internal and external
- each contact with a customer is a moment of truth
- once you know what the customer needs, wants and expects, satisfy them
- do something extra every time
- set measurable standards and monitor them
- handle complaints well
- always put yourself in the customer's shoes.

APPENDIX

EXPECTATIONS

- professionalism
- caring
- honest
- polite
- information
- helpful
- cheerful
- the product or service you want/need
- hassle free
- efficient
- good value
- prompt
- attentive
- respectful
- sensitive

WORKING WITH MANAGEMENT

WHAT MAKES MANAGERS TICK?

In a world of continuous change the needs of management have not changed much over the years. They still need responsibility and challenges in order to be motivated and successful. They still seek to have a strong team to support them and help them to achieve these successes. It is all of these things that actually makes a manager tick and strive for continuous growth.

So, if strong support is one of the factors that contribute to a manager's success then you, as an individual, have a big part to play in contributing to that success. You are assisting management to do the job. This is all very well when working on a one-to-one basis, however, the one-to-one relationship is not so common nowadays. You may report directly to one person but also be providing support to others. This has a lot to do with the current business climate and restructures and flatter structures within organisations. However, the role of someone in any Administrative Support position is increasingly becoming more demanding and requires the same skills and qualities. The main difference is that secretaries may be working for three or more managers and other administrative staff may be working in larger teams.

WHAT DOES THIS MEAN?

It means a heavier workload, greater involvement and responsibility, and perhaps taking on some management responsibilities yourself.

What an opportunity for those of you in these positions! However, you may still be struggling to manage your own time effectively, to prioritise and plan workloads, to communicate effectively, to create a professional image for yourself, your team and your organisation. Generally, to ensure the smooth operation of the department. Of course, having to do all of these things makes the working day hectic and often quite stressful.

Here are three headings that will help you to do your jobs even more effectively and feel truly involved in your role. These are suggestions – there is no one right way of doing things – what works for one may not work for another. Nevertheless, the following will start your brains ticking and perhaps help you to assess your situation and look more objectively at the team and where you fit in. These headings are:

- Understanding managers' priorities.

- Communicating with the manager.

- Building up a good working relationship.

UNDERSTANDING MANAGERS' PRIORITIES

In order for you to plan and prioritise your day you need to know and understand the priorities of the people you work with.

The benefits of understanding are:

- you will understand *why* you do things

- you will gain information

- you can set your own priorities

- you can use your initiative by knowing what is ahead

- you can do some research for manager(s)

- you can chase deadlines on behalf of manager(s)

Most managers will have clear objectives and targets set out for them and their teams on a yearly or six monthly basis. You need to know these as you are a key part of helping the manager to achieve those objectives. However, just knowing these objectives isn't enough. There are other details you should be aware of in order for you to understand what needs to be done. These might include:

- the deadline by which each target needs to be achieved
- the people involved in achieving the targets (might not just be your manager(s))
- who is actually doing what.

There are various ways you can find out objectives:

- simply by asking your managers and colleagues
- reading their development plans
- attending team meetings.

Sometimes managers don't see the need for an administrative member of the team to attend team meetings. However, you are a member of the team not adjunct to it. There are enormous benefits in attending team meetings that will help you to assess and plan priorities for yourself and the people you work with.

These will include:

- becoming more involved and getting background information
- learning about short term objectives
- finding out why the team is taking a certain route to achieve targets
- finding out who is doing what and by when.

You, of course, will be able to keep notes of deadlines and anticipate work ahead.

EXAMPLE:

Your manager has decided to have a team meeting to review the procedures within the department. You attend the meeting as part of the team. The aim and objective is to discuss drills and procedures with a result of producing a manual with all 50 procedures in written form. Your manager is chairing the meeting and their target is to have the manual produced in six months. They will delegate a certain amount to each team member to review and write each procedure by a different date. Some will take longer than others. This is your opportunity to make a note of who is doing what and by when so that you are well informed. Perhaps you can also take on some of the procedures yourself.

COMMUNICATING WITH YOUR MANAGER

We usually communicate with people for a purpose, to give/receive information. It is no different when communicating with the manager. You may feel that because you see your manager(s) almost every day there is no need for structured communication. However, this is not the case. If you depend on communicating with your manager as they pass through the office going to and from meetings, clients visits etc., you will not get all of the information you need in order to do the job. Also, you may not work in the same office as your manager in which case relying on asking them when you see them will not be very effective. You need to ensure that the people you work with take the time to explain, inform and tell you what's going on.

Structure your communication. That means planning and diarying a 'one-to-one' (1:1) with your manager. These 1:1s will help you to do the job effectively. Make sure you have at least one a month. Ask your manager for 1:1's – do not wait for them to be offered. At your 1:1 discuss your performance at work last month, your targets and work for the coming months plus any difficulties you have faced and any successes you have had. You should not use this time as an opportunity to have a general whinge. Ideally, half an hour should be long enough. Do make sure you let your manager know anything that they can do to help you to be more effective at work.

To set up 1:1's:

- Suggest to your manager that there are certain things that you need to do the job effectively. Say that by introducing this structured communication you are saving time for each other by using the 1:1s to get details and background information for tasks that need to be done and by looking at priorities you will both know that important tasks will be done first.

- Put the 1:1s in the diary six months ahead and treat them as 'sacred'. Discipline yourself to stick to them and remind yourself and your manager of the importance of effective communication.
Remember you are saving time long term.

It is a good idea to plan 1:1's with people other than your manager. For example, people you work with on particular tasks. You need to communicate with them for the same reasons as your manager. They will need to give you background information when a task is set. So, regular structured communication with the people you work with is necessary.

BUILDING UP A GOOD WORKING RELATIONSHIP

We have already talked about knowing your manager's objectives in order to understand priorities, and effective communication in order to plan, prioritise and save time. By doing these things you will be one step ahead of your manager at all times, and you have a basis to build up a good working relationship.

When dealing with your manager put yourself into their shoes. People have very high expectations of bosses, which, because they are human beings, they can't always meet.

People, including managers, are influenced by what has happened to them in the past. Your perception of work is based on what your personal experience has been. For example, if your manager is used to working for a hierarchical, autocratic organisation they will probably approach managing you in an autocratic way. This is not necessarily their fault. Make sure you know how your boss sees you. Don't make assumptions. Ask them at your next appraisal or 1:1 and ask them to be honest with you. If you feel you can't ask, then look for clues in their behaviour. eg:

- if your manager gets impatient with you it may be that you are whinging or they feel your complaints are unconstructive

- if your manager reacts aggressively towards you it may be that you have behaved aggressively towards them

- does your manager actively seek out your views and opinions? If they don't it may be because you have not responded positively and supportively in the past.

It there is a problem, before you blame the manager, ask yourself if you were in any way to blame.

However, the everyday systems, drills and routines are equally as important in building up this working relationship. So too is the way you deal with people and situations.

INFORMATION AND QUESTIONING

Know about your manager, the team, and the organisation. Read the literature that is available to you. Ask questions when you don't understand. You are not expected to know or understand everything first time round and, of course, it won't always be communicated clearly. You may be afraid to ask questions for fear you will look foolish. However, you will be none the wiser for holding back.

> 'He who asks a question is a fool for a moment and he who never asks a question is a fool for life'.
> CONFUCIUS

Ask open questions that will require more than a yes/no answer:

Open Questions

What	Who
Why	Which
Where	How
When	

EXAMPLE:

Your manager has just returned from an important meeting and you wish to find out what actions have been taken that will affect you and your workload.

CLOSED

Q. How was the meeting?
A. Fine

OPEN

Q. What are the actions as a result of the meeting?

This question will give you all of the information you need. People will respect you more for asking questions when you don't understand rather than going away unsure and doing the job wrong.

ORGANISING YOURSELF

You will read all about the importance of planning in the Time Management Chapter. I would like to stress again the importance of taking time at the beginning of each day to plan and prioritise your day. Using a list to do this and ensuring the important tasks are done first, nothing is forgotten and doing one task at a time. Be proactive and keep thinking ahead.

EXAMPLE:

You may have responsibility for organising the organisation's Annual General Meeting. You will know well in advance all of the things that need to be done for the conference. Again, in the Time Management Chapter you will read about the importance of using checklists when organising events of any kind. Some of the tasks will need to be done months in advance, i.e. invitations, programme etc. Other tasks will be done right up to the day of the conference.

You can organise yourself and your diary around this. Set yourself a plan including all of the tasks that need to be done for the conference, leaving some space to do other normal day to day tasks. Explain to your managers and colleagues that the conference will take priority the weeks leading up to it. Remember the success of it will depend heavily upon you.

ESTABLISHING THE GROUND RULES:

It is important that you establish the ground rules with the people you work with. They will appreciate it when you sit down and ask them what they expect of you. You can

also tell them some of the things you expect from them in order to do your job.

If you are a secretary some of the issues you might discuss are:

- who is going to control the diary?

- can you make appointments on behalf of your managers?

- who will open the post?

- will you be drafting letters on behalf of your managers?

- ask your managers to put a date/deadline on all work given to you – *not* urgent/a.s.a.p.

- how often will you have one-to-ones?

By establishing the ground rules you will have a common understanding. The problems occur when this hasn't happened and you don't know what is expected of you or when people expect things but haven't said so.

Don't be afraid to be open and honest with the people you work with. By doing this you will build respect and trust and a healthy working relationship. They will confide in you, ask you for advice and keep you involved. Praise people when you feel a task has been done well and be honest when things could have been achieved a better way. Hopefully, they will do the same with you.

In reality, things do not always go the way we want them to or according to plan, but focus on the solution rather that the problem when things go wrong. Managers will appreciate this.

> **EXAMPLE:**
>
> On the day of the Annual General Conference a group of the guests turn up at the wrong building because they haven't received the correct instructions. Rather than focusing on the problem (i.e. who sent out the instructions etc.) focus on the situation. Arrange for the guests to be taxied to the venue as quickly as possible. Be there to greet them and to apologise for the situation and take them to join the other guests.

After the conference when you are evaluating the day, looking at what went well or didn't go so well, you can think about how you can ensure a situation like that doesn't arise again.

PUBLIC RELATIONS AND CREATING A PROFESSIONAL IMAGE

You are often the first point of contact when meeting people face-to-face or speaking with people on the telephone. 'You never get a second chance to create a first impression', therefore, the image you create when dealing with people is important.

The image you portray will also reflect on your organisation, so you will want to create the best image possible. Here are some tips for creating a professional impression:

- check your posture
- smile, look interested and listen
- expression both vocal and facial
- speech – say the right things clearly and openly
- eagerness – offer help, suggestions and advice.

The right appearance is important because a potential client/customer can be put off by someone who looks too 'way out' or scruffy. Similarly your manager will take you more seriously if you look the part as well as acting it. The right clothes can create confidence in the wearer's ability to do the job and do it well. There is an argument that says that if someone can do a job then it should not matter about their appearance. However it is also true that casual clothes such as jeans create a 'relaxed' feeling in the mind of the wearer and this should not be allowed to influence attitudes at work. If you wish to be taken seriously then you must look the part and dress in a business-like way.

Remember, style is not fashion. It is all about developing you as an individual, wearing what suits you best and putting across the best possible impression.

SUMMARY

- know the objectives of the people you work with
- have regular 1:1's with the people you work with
- ask questions and read all information available to you
- have effective systems and drills
- organise yourself, be pro-active and plan ahead
- establish the ground rules with your manager
- be open and honest
- focus on solutions not problems
- create the best image possible for yourself and your organisation
- look smart — this shows determination and self-confidence.

HANDLING YOUR APPRAISAL

WHAT IS APPRAISAL?

An appraisal is a yearly meeting that you have with your manager where you discuss your performance in your job last year and set targets for the coming year. Some organisations appraise their staff on a six monthly basis, but most do it yearly.

Appraisal is important to an organisation because it is a means of identifying how satisfied and how well people are doing in their jobs. It enables target setting to either develop them or improve their current performance and provides the opportunity to motivate individuals and get their commitment to the aims and objectives of the organisation.

The objective of an appraisal is therefore 'to *help improve individual performance, realise potential and achieve better results for the organisation*'.

Your appraisal will be concerned with three main areas:

- a review of your past performance, from which lessons can be learned for your future performance

- an identification of your future needs, and linking those into the needs of your department and organisation

- identifying an action plan which specifies what has to be done, by who and by when.

BENEFITS OF APPRAISAL

TO YOU

- finding out how well you are doing in your job compared to what is expected of you

- talking about what opportunities there are in your current job to develop your potential

- talking about what opportunities may crop up in the future and what you can be doing to prepare yourself

- identifying any training needs you might have

- identifying what your strengths and weaknesses are and what you can do to improve on them

- clarifying your job objectives and direction.

TO YOUR MANAGER/ORGANISATION

- identifying your talent and potential

- identifying your training and development needs

- discussing your career ambitions

- identifying your strengths and weaknesses

- clarifying what standards of performance are expected from you and setting targets for either development or improvement.

KEY REQUIREMENTS OF AN EFFECTIVE APPRAISAL

For your appraisal to be effective it is important that it is carried out by your immediate boss and that both of you have thoroughly prepared for it.

You should concentrate 70% of the time on the future and only 30% on the past. This is because you can only really use the past to learn from and you can do nothing to change it. However, you can do a lot to change how you handle your job in the future.

You must be clear about what your standards of performance are and what is expected of you on a daily basis. You should also ensure that you have regular 1:1s with your manager. (A 1:1 is a monthly half hour meeting that you have with your manager which is a bit like a 'mini' appraisal. At the 1:1 you discuss your performance over the last month and your targets and expected performance for the coming month.)

An appraisal should never be used as an opportunity to discipline someone or for you to have a general 'whinge'.

STANDARDS OF PERFORMANCE

A standard of performance relating to the job is a continuing yardstick for judging whether your performance is at an acceptable level. It should be realistic, measurable and recognisable. Standards will relate to the job itself, regardless of who is carrying out that job, and never to the individual.

Standards of performance are important because an organisation must ensure that it is consistent in the goods and/or services that it provides for its customers.

Some jobs lend themselves very well to measurable standards, (eg sales people) while others may involve recognised methods of good practice.

The six ways of considering how to answer the question *'What are the standards of performance expected of me?'* are as follows:

- NUMERIC   sales figures
  production levels
  defect levels
  error rates
  paper flow

- DEADLINES   projects
  turnaround of paper
  statutory

	regular meetings dates
	answering the phone
● FINANCIAL	working within budgets
	sales figures
	keeping within expenditure
	profit figures
● PROCEDURAL	stages of writing a computer
	programme
	internal liaison systems
	timings on replying to
	customer complaints
	giving out information
● NEGATIVE	number of complaints
	feedback from colleagues
● RECOGNISABLE	approach to customers
	presentation at meetings
	typing errors/house style
	dress
	housekeeping

Before going in to your appraisal, make sure that you know what standards of performance are expected of you and how well you have been doing against them. If there are any that you are unsure of, this will be a good opportunity to clarify them. If your boss is unclear about what your standards should be, set your own, write them down and give them to the boss.

TARGET SETTING

A target is a priority over and above your normal work. Targets are about change and development and relate to the individual, ie, to you, and *not* to the job, although clearly they are often linked to your job.

Targets are set:

- to achieve better results
- to get you to give your best performance
- to develop your skills, abilities and knowledge
- to provide a challenge and a sense of achievement
- to improve communication between you and your boss.

Targets are a good part of an appraisal system and will help you to improve your performance as well as give you an opportunity to develop new skills. You should discuss your targets with your manager and make sure that they are challenging, ie, not something that you can very easily do, but something that will stretch you a little. Make sure that you have no more than six targets at any one time and be sure that you know exactly what is expected of you and by when. Get them written down.

EXAMPLES OF STANDARDS AND TARGETS

Key Result Area	Standard of performance	Target
Secretary Correspondence	Deal with correspondence within 48 hours	Reduce errors to not more than 2.5% by 31 Dec
Filing clerk Invoice files	Filing to be done on a daily basis	Clear backlog of unfiled invoices by 25/9
Salesperson Patch maintenance and development	Call rate to average 8 per day at average 18 miles per call	To gain 3 new clients in October at minimum of £800 per month

Scientist Research	To produce at least 3 research papers per year	Attend July conference on NLP – report in Sept
Social worker Battered child cases	In category A cases visiting to be every 2 weeks followed by report to supervisor	Report on social case meeting 'X' at weekly intervals during May

PREPARING FOR YOUR APPRAISAL

In order for your appraisal to be most effective it is important that you are fully prepared for it. This means that ideally, throughout the year, you are collecting bits of information that will be useful to you during your appraisal.

Set up a personal file for yourself in which you keep copies of everything that relates to your performance at work. For example, copies of your previous appraisals, 'happy' letters from customers, a piece of work that you completed that you are particularly proud of, a problem you sorted out and so on.

Make sure that you have also kept a written record of targets that you have met as well as your personal achievements.

You should also identify in advance of your appraisal interview the following:

- what parts of your job have you particularly enjoyed in the past year?

- what parts have given you the most difficulty?

- what particular successes have you had during the last year?

- are there any constraints or problems which have adversely affected your performance?
- do you feel your manager has in any way restricted your ability to do your job?
- what do you consider to be your major strengths?
- are you sure of your exact authority?
- are the boundaries of your job clear?
- do you receive enough information on an ongoing basis about your performance?
- what are your career ambitions?
- are your abilities being fully used in your current job?
- what specific help could you be given by
    training
    colleagues
    management?

Ensure that before your appraisal interview you have read your job description and noted down where what you currently do differs from what is written down.

Make yourself feel more confident for your appraisal by dressing smartly. Ensure that you turn up at the venue on time and well prepared and bring with you any documentation you want to show your manager.

YOUR CHECKLIST FOR YOUR INTERVIEW

1 Are you sure of the exact boundaries of your job?

- is there any overlap – two people believing that they are responsible for a certain area of work?

- is there any uncertainty – areas where you are not absolutely sure whether this item is your responsibility at all?

- are there areas not covered – areas for which no one seems to take any responsibility?

2 Are your sure of your exact authority?

- what are the limits of authority in each area of work?

- are these limits high enough or too high?

- in what areas are decisions left to your discretion?

- in what areas do you need more room to use your discretion?

- in what areas would you like more room to use your discretion?

3 What level of performance have you reached in each of the areas of your accountability and against your targets?

- money – is the departmental budget reasonable, too high or too low?

- administrative resources – is the equipment satisfactory to do the job?

- communication – do you have adequate warning of changes? Sufficient information on matters affecting the work? Communication of management thinking?

- what other knowledge would help you in your work?

- is there sufficient liaison between other departments, ie, those to whom you pass work and those from whom you receive work?

> • are there any other difficulties that hamper you, eg, lack of space, poor floor planning, awkward access, lack of prompt attention to maintenance of machines etc?
>
> 4 Do you have adequate information on your progress towards targets?
>
> 5 What specific assistance can be given to help you?

THE 6 STAGES OF AN APPRAISAL INTERVIEW

1 REVIEW LAST YEAR'S PERFORMANCE

- identify achievements against targets
- identify strengths and weaknesses
- be positive.

2 DISCUSS THE JOB

- check areas of responsibility and limits of authority
- where can improvements be made?

3 FACE UP TO PROBLEM AREAS

- examine any areas of disagreement between you
- be specific and factual, focussing on results.

4 AGREE A PLAN OF ACTION

- to correct/improve weaknesses

- put forward ideas
- agree a plan.

5 TALK ABOUT THE FUTURE

- talk about your career aspirations
- agree targets for achievements
- decide on any help/training you need.

6 MONITORING

- agree the monitoring process
- end on a positive note and thank your manager.

SUMMARY

- Prepare for your appraisal thoroughly. Collect all relevant information and take it with you to the appraisal.

- At your appraisal, concentrate on future targets rather than past performance.

- Ensure you come out of the appraisal with specific targets to meet, with deadlines and standards attached.

CAREER DEVELOPMENT

Career development is not necessarily about being promoted or becoming a Managing Director. It can simply be about trying to extend your skills so that you are the best at the job that you already do, or moving sideways into a different field.

With any plans for career development, it is important that you identify where you are now and where you want to be.

WHERE YOU ARE NOW

- what do you like about your current job?

- what do you dislike?

- what qualities/strengths do you bring to this job?

- what weaknesses do you have that make the job difficult?

- what new skills/experiences are you gaining from this job?

- what further training or development do you need that will help you to be more effective in your current job?

WHERE DO YOU WANT TO BE?

Imagine that you are attending your retirement party and that your bosses, colleagues and team members are all giving a speech about you and your career. What would you want them to say about you? This will help you to begin to clarify what is important to you in terms of your career. Write the speeches for them **now**. Don't write down what you have already achieved. Write down what you think you would like to have achieved by the time you come to retirement.

It doesn't matter if you are not absolutely clear about what you want to do in the long term. You can, nonetheless, begin to identify certain things that you **do** know.

Now make a list of all the things that you do want to do. Then break these goals down into achievable chunks.

eg:

GOAL	TIME SCALE
Become the manager of a sales unit	Within next 5 years
• *Attend management training course*	*Within next 2 years*
• *Have the best sales record in the unit*	*By end of the sales year*
Become proficient at budgeting	Within next 2 years
• *Ask my boss to delegate some of next year's budgeting to me*	*By end of this month*
• *Get qualification in accounting year*	*By end of next*

The smaller you break each stage in to, the more likely you are to achieve your goal. Make sure that you always set yourself time scales against each smaller goal.

When identifying your goals, make sure that you are clear as to exactly **why** it is you want to achieve them. Once you are sure of the answer why, you will be clearer about how realistic the goal is or if there are some other things that you need to do in order to achieve it.

SWOT ANALYSIS

A SWOT analysis is an analysis of your strengths, weaknesses, opportunities and threats. It is basically a way of identifying which areas you need to work on in order to be successful.

For example

STRENGTHS
7 years experience of sales

Attention to detail
Good working relationship with boss

WEAKNESSES
Poor sales record last month
Impatient
Don't get on well with Accounts Department

OPPORTUNITIES
New product coming out next month
Staff Christmas 'do' coming up
Attending successful selling course next month

THREATS
Fred and Mildred have consistently higher sales
records than me
Our company's market share has dropped by 10%

Ask a friend or a close colleague to add to it or to
comment on it so that you are getting another perspective.

Then TAKE ACTION. What can you do to maximise
your strengths, improve on your weaknesses, grasp the
opportunities and minimise the threats?

MOVING UP THE ORGANISATION

If one of your career aims is to be promoted within your
organisation there are three areas that you need to
concentrate on.

- developing yourself

- getting to know people

- demonstrating your ability

DEVELOPING YOURSELF

The higher up the organisation that you move, the more you will be required to have a breadth of skills greater than simply your technical skills.

If you imagine an organisation looking like the envelope below.

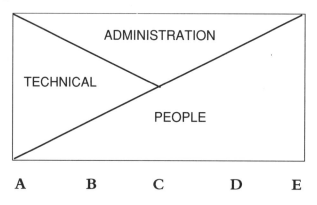

At point A you are likely to be 'front line staff', in other words, in a non-managerial position concentrating purely on your own work. At point B you are likely to be a first line manager who still has some responsibility for 'technical' work, that is, involved directly in the outcome of the department, but a lot of your time will be taken in up in administration and managing people. At point C, you are likely to be a middle manager and you will spend very little time producing work yourself. Most of your time at that level will be dealing with administration and managing other people's work. At point D, you will be a senior manager with much less administration to do, no technical work and a lot of managing people responsibilities. At point E, you are likely to be a Managing Director with no technical work, no administrative work. You will spend nearly all of your time managing the people in your organisation and deciding policy.

What all the above effectively means is that if you want to move into a managerial position, you need to ensure that you are broadening your skill base into areas other than your current 'technical' job.

For example, if at the moment you are an accounts clerk and you want to become a manager, it is not enough to simply be a very good accounts clerk. You will need to find out about and have an understanding of sales and possibly marketing.

So the first step to progressing your career is to DEVELOP yourself.

To prepare yourself for a more senior position you need to:

- attend relevant training courses. Put into action what you have learned

- read your organisation's annual report

- get involved in internal projects, particularly those that ask for volunteers

- get further education by either attending courses at your local college or going for distance learning where you study at home. If you possibly can, turn that further learning into a further qualification by either studying for an O' Level, A' Level, degree or even an NVQ (details of names and addresses of where to go to find out about further education and NVQs can be found at the end of this chapter).

- take a secondment for a few days, weeks or months to another department so that you can find out how people operate in different parts of the organisation

- read magazines, trade journals, books relevant to your organisation or trade

- watch the news. Read quality newspapers. Broaden your general knowledge

- don't wait for your boss to offer to develop you. Go and ask for further training and development.

- ask your boss to delegate some of their work to you so that you can find out more about what they do and what you need to learn more about in order to progress

- get involved in training other people in an area of work that you are particularly skilled at

- attend any organisational social gatherings and functions. This is a really good way to get to know people and for them to get to know you. Also, it is a lot easier to talk to people who are perhaps senior to you in an informal situation rather than a formal one.

- try and find out what other departments in the organisation do. What are their priorities and what are their problems?

- apply for jobs to demonstrate your keenness to get on. Get some practice at being interviewed.

GET TO KNOW THE RIGHT PEOPLE

It is really important in an organisation to make sure that you know the people who are going to be in a position to help you progress and that they know you.

This is not 'creeping' or 'sucking up' to senior people. It is plain common sense. Quite apart from anything else, it is not necessarily senior people who can help you progress. If you have really impressed someone junior in another department and they then mention to their boss how good you are at your job, you are increasing your chances of progressing in the organisation.

Imagine that you are appointing a child minder. You have a choice between a childminder that a friend of yours uses and speaks very highly of and who you have met a couple of times and liked their approach to handling children, and an applicant who looks very impressive on paper but who you have never met. Common sense would dictate that you are likely to choose the one that you know about and have heard good reports about than the one who you don't know where you would be taking a risk.

Although the analogy may seem somewhat spurious, it is actually extremely apt, because it is the same at work.

If you want to appoint someone to a really important job and you are faced with a choice between an applicant that you know of, whom has impressed other people in the organisation and whose work you have some knowledge of and some one whom you have never met, never heard of but who looks good on paper, you are much more likely to choose the one that you have heard about. Common sense.

This does not mean that you have to be fake friendly to people that you don't like very much. What it means is that no matter what the provocation, you need to be unfailingly courteous, civil, helpful and professional to EVERYONE in the organisation, even the people that you don't have much time for.

- speak to everyone in the organisation as if they were equal and of the same level of importance as the Managing Director or Chief Executive

- when anyone asks you for your help, make every effort to assist. If you can't help them immediately, tell them when you can. If you can't help at all, explain why politely and offer to help next time

- thank people if they have helped you, both verbally and if appropriate, by memo

- if you are expected to attend meetings, make sure that you turn up on time and well prepared

- approach **every** situation with a positive attitude

- don't be cynical. It isn't productive and it doesn't help for people to have a high opinion of you and your abilities

- if you are asked your views, be honest. Don't tell people what you think they want to hear

- present problems and complaints constructively and objectively. When going to your boss with a problem take in at least one possible solution.

DEMONSTRATE YOUR ABILITY

You need to let people know how capable you are. Don't expect them to simply 'know'.

This means doing the best you can at whatever you are asked to do.

- draw your boss's attention to the successes of your colleagues as well as yourself

- don't be afraid to ask questions

- make appointments to see your boss to discuss particular issues

- find yourself a mentor. Someone more senior than you in the organisation with whom you can talk over issues and problems and who will give you honest feedback

- don't get involved in office politics. Don't take sides. Formulate your own view. Don't immediately take the view of the person who is 'telling you the story', they may only be seeing it from one side and there are always two sides to any situation. Don't get involved in backbiting and pettinesses, although it is very easy to do

- find someone in the organisation who you admire and think highly of and emulate what they do

- do the best you can at your own job. Don't avoid tasks that you don't enjoy doing.

When you are faced with a situation at work there are three things that you can do. You can complain at great length and upset yourself further and anyone within earshot. You can accept the fact that there is nothing that you can do to change whatever it is and keep quiet and just get on with it. Or you can try to do something about it.

Clearly the second and third options are the most positive way of tackling things that you are unhappy about.

'God, give me the courage to change the things I can change, the strength to accept the things I cannot change and the wisdom to know the difference'.

BEING PREPARED

There is undoubtedly an element of luck in any kind of career progression. Sometimes you end up in situations or fields of work quite by chance. However, luck is useless to you unless you are prepared and ready to seize the opportunity that has presented itself to you.

This means that you should live your career life as if at any moment you are going to be offered an opportunity to progress or develop, whether that is up or sideways.

A famous sports personality once said to a reporter who suggested that his success had been primarily due to good luck 'That may be true, but I have found that the harder I practice the luckier I get!'

So, you need to be prepared and ready to grasp your opportunities when they present themselves, which they undoubtedly will.

- Your appearance is crucial. Unfair though it may be, first impressions really count, either for you or against you. Dress in the way that best suits the job that you want to be in rather than the job that you are in currently.

- Ensure that you approach people and situations with commitment, enthusiasm and professionalism. Treat all people you encounter at work, whether internal or external, as important. Their rank and status should not affect very much how you behave towards them.

- When you commit yourself to achieving a task or a deadline, stick to it.

- Fight hard for what you believe is right, but be prepared to give way in the face of stronger arguments.

- Be friendly to people.

- LISTEN!! Remember that you have 2 ears and 1 mouth. Use them in those proportions.

- Respect other's views and strengths. If someone is better than you at performing a particular function, acknowledge it and learn from them.

- Take responsibility for more than just your own job.

- Use your time to improve.

- Admit your mistakes in an open and honest way.

- Always focus on possibilities and solutions.

HOW TO BE SUCCESSFUL AT INTERVIEWS

If you are presented with an opportunity for promotion, or indeed even going to work for another organisation you will be judged as much on how you conduct yourself at the interview as on your past job experience and performance.

The key to having a successful interview is PREPARATION.

PREPARATION

- Research thoroughly everything you can about the job, the department and if it's an external job you're applying for, the organisation.

- Speak to the person who currently holds the job. Find out exactly what it entails, what they like and dislike about it.

- In a notebook, make notes of all the information that you have found out.

- In your notebook, write down a minimum of 10

questions that you can ask at the interview. It is important to have at least 10, because the chances are that many of the questions you want to ask will be answered before you have the chance to ask them. You want to make sure that you have a least a couple to ask.

- Try to find out what kinds of questions you are likely to be asked at the interview. If no one can tell you then use your common sense. Put yourself into the shoes of the interviewer and imagine what sorts of questions you would ask if you were the one conducting the interview.

- Note down your answers to possible questions in your notebook.

- Type up a brief description of your major achievements. Things that probably wouldn't be on your CV, for example, successful pieces of work that you have done etc.

- Dress in the style that fits the job that you are applying for, not the one that you are currently in.

DURING THE INTERVIEW

- Take your notebook in with you and make notes during the interview.

- Use your notebook as a reference point. If you are asked a question and you need time to think about your answer, then refer to your notes.

- If the interviewer asks you a question that you had written down, cross it off your list in your notebook. Do it in an obvious way so that the interviewer can see how thoroughly you have prepared.

- Take your time answering questions.

- Don't feel that you have to have an answer for every question. Waffling is nearly always obvious. If you don't know the answer then say so.

- At the end of the interview run through your notes and make sure that you have said everything you wanted to.

AFTER THE INTERVIEW

- Send a letter to the interviewer thanking them for the interview. Even if you don't get the job, at the very least you have gained valuable interview experience and raised your profile.

SUMMARY

- Identify where you are and where you want to be
- Be clear about your strengths and weaknesses
- Develop yourself
- Get to know the right people
- Prepare thoroughly for interviews

USEFUL ADDRESSES AND TELEPHONE NUMBERS

RSA Examinations Board
Westwood Way
Coventry CV4 8HS
Tel: 0203 470033

Open University
Parsifal College
527 Finchley Road
London NW3 7BG
Tel: 071 794 0575

City & Guilds
46 Britannia Street
London WC1X 9RG
Tel: 071 278 2468

The Industrial Society
Peter Runge House
3 Carlton House Terrace
London SW1Y 5AF
Tel: 071 839 4300
      (Head Office)
      021 454 6769
      (Course Bookings Unit)

**Pitmans Education and
Training Ltd**
154 Southampton Row
London WC1B 5AX
Tel: 071 837 4481
      (Course Enquiries)
      071 278 6877
      (Administration)

**National Extension
College**
18 Brooklands
Cambridge CB2 2HN
Tel: 0223 316644

TIME MANAGEMENT

Effective time management is simply about self discipline. There are no magic formulas, no pieces of paper to fill in which will suddenly make you good at managing your time.

Everyone has a lot of work to do and not enough time in which to do it. However, we can all think of people who seem very organised and others who seem very disorganised. Both kinds have the same amounts of work to do, but the first kind manage it better.

The first lesson to learn about time management is that in the real world of work, things go wrong. Computers break down, files go missing, problems crop up and so on. These things will **always** happen and there is really no way of avoiding them. What you can do however is **plan** for them. This means developing and using a simple set of time management systems that work for you.

Before you can start to plan on what and when you spend your time you need to know how much you have available to you. Managing and budgeting your time is very similar to how you manage and budget your money. Imagine your salary. At the end of each month you are paid a sum which you know about in advance. You therefore know how much you can afford to spend on things like mortgages, bills, food, clothes etc. If in any given month you receive a particularly large bill you adjust your money accordingly. You may choose not to go out for dinner for instance, or not to put money away to save. You can do this because you know exactly what your income and expenditure is.

You also know exactly how much time you have available to you. That is, 60 minutes in an hour, 24 hours in a day and so on. The amount of time there is is static. You also usually know how long you have to complete any particular task, because most tasks have deadlines.

So, once you know this you can start budgeting your time, just as you would budget your money.

IDENTIFYING YOUR PRIORITIES

To balance your time, you need to know what your priorities are. With your salary, you know that a priority is your mortgage or rent, therefore you will ensure that you have enough money to pay for that. Similarly with time, you need to ensure that you are spending it on your priorities.

To identify your priorities you need to know

- What is the purpose of your job? What are you expected to achieve and in what time scale?

- What do you need to do (which tasks do you need to carry out) in order to achieve that purpose?

The answers to the above questions are your priorities. When deciding which task to tackle first, remind yourself of your purpose. For example, if you are short of time, you should perhaps deal with the customer's query rather than write the internal report.

- Make a summary of your job. Write down all the things that you believe you are expected to achieve and take it to your boss to discuss. This will help both you, and your boss, to be clear as to exactly what you are expected to achieve. It will also help to clear up any previous misunderstandings.

MANAGING YOUR PRIORITIES

There are effectively two categories into which work falls, those tasks which are REACTIVE and those which are PROACTIVE.

Reactive tasks are those that are an immediate response to something. Proactive tasks are those that you know about in advance and can therefore plan for.

- You need to know roughly what percentage of your working day and week you spend on either proactive or reactive tasks. So, if you discover that you spend approximately 70% of your working day on proactive tasks and 30% on reactive tasks then you only plan 70% of work for that day and leave 30% of your time free. That way, when the inevitable happens and something goes wrong or you get interrupted, you will still have achieved what you set out to, that is, 70% of your proactive tasks.

- One of the most common mistakes that people make in managing their priorities is that they leave the 'big' and important tasks until last while they clear up all the 'little' jobs. Of course, what normally happens is that they get to the end of the day and realise they have spent all day on relatively unimportant tasks and interruptions and then feel stressed because they still have the important jobs to do.

- Never leave things until the last minute. Plan in the time that you intend to spend on a certain job and stick to it.

THE DIARY

The diary is one of the resources you have to help you. Most people only use diaries to plan meetings, appointments, holidays etc. This is a wasteful use of the diary. The diary can also be used to help you plan and manage your priorities.

- Use your diary to make appointments with yourself to do tasks. This will help you to manage your proactive and reactive time better and allow you to build in time in a realistic and workable way for things to go wrong.

For example, you have a report to do that is due in on Thursday lunch time. If you choose to do the report on Tuesday you give yourself a full day spare if something should go wrong. Ideally the report would only take you one hour to complete, however, given that you are bound to be interrupted or something is likely to happen, you should allow yourself at least an hour and a half. So, in your diary make an appointment at say, 2.30pm to do the report. Schedule the next task for 4.00pm. This way you have actually created more time for yourself, because if all goes well and you actually complete the report without interruptions, you will have gained half an hour in your day to do something else with. Even if you are interrupted, you are likely to have completed the report within the time scale you set yourself.

Remember, that given the opportunity to estimate how much time a job is going to take, people will nearly always underestimate. Using a diary in this way will help you to make more sensible decisions about how to allocate time to others and also about agreeing to deadlines that you can realistically meet without affecting the rest of your work.

MANAGING DEADLINES

Imagine that you have been asked by your boss to meet a deadline. You argue and protest but eventually give way and agree to the deadline, knowing that in reality you won't be able to meet it. You may use the well known escape phrase 'I'll try' because you can't convince the boss otherwise, or simply because it is the boss, an important customer or a colleague and you don't want to be seen to be unhelpful. Then, as you *knew* you would, you miss the deadline. What your boss/customer/colleague will remember is **not** that you protested loudly at the time of the deadline, but that you didn't meet a deadline that you had agreed to.

- Instead of giving in to a deadline that you know you cannot meet, you should stand your ground. Say that you cannot meet that particular deadline, explain the reason why and then offer an alternative deadline that you are confident that you can meet. Although at the time your boss/customer/colleague may feel that you are not co-operating with them, what they will remember about you in the long run is that you meet deadlines that you have agreed to.

- If you explain WHY you can't meet the deadline and WHEN you can do the task they are asking you to do people are much more likely to understand and accept your refusal. But you must always offer an alternative deadline.

- Delete the letters ASAP from your vocabulary. Piles of paper marked ASAP are meaningless. If you have a lot of paperwork to deal with all marked ASAP you have no way of knowing which one is the most important and therefore should be done first.

- When sending out paperwork or leaving messages, always give an actual date and if necessary, time, when you need it done by. Similarly, if you receive a document marked ASAP, contact the sender to find out exactly when they need it done by. How often have you had someone ask you to do something 'as soon as possible' and when you've said 'Will next Friday do', they've replied 'Good heavens, no! I need it by next Tuesday at the latest!'

For example: '*Please can you let me have the completed form back by 19 November. I need it to complete my monthly returns which I need to send to Accounts by 30 November*'.

- Never leave it to the last minute to chase someone if there is a deadline. You **know** that you haven't received it, it's likely that it hasn't been done. So by chasing at the time of the deadline you are creating a situation where you feel annoyed, the other person feel harassed and you are both likely to walk away from the encounter with negative thoughts about one another.

- Chase up people in advance of deadlines. Do it politely by using a phrase such as 'Just checking to see if there are any problems.' Better still, let people know in advance that you will be ringing them to see how they are getting on. Say something like 'I'll call the day before to see if there are any problems.' Very few people will be offended by that. In fact they are much more likely to welcome it.

ROLLING 'TO DO' LIST

A rolling 'to do' list is basically a diary or book which is dated. Instead of writing down a daily list of things to do, or a weekly one and moving things from one list to the other, write down what you have to do on the day on which you intend to do it. This is similar to the diary system, except that you write in the diary the *big jobs*, appointments to produce reports and so on. In your rolling 'to do' book you write the little jobs, for example, telephone Mavis Turtle, arrange team meeting venue etc. This system will help you to make sensible decisions about making better use of you time. Don't have more than eight things to do in one day. You won't have time to do them all. Any additional tasks should be moved or planned for following days.

EVERYTHING BOOK

An Everything Book is an A4 hardback book that you carry around with you everywhere. Anything at all that you have to write down, from minutes of meetings to telephone messages or telephone numbers is all written in one book. This way you only have to look in one place for notes of numbers and meetings etc. You will never be searching the wastepaper bin or the trays on your desk for important pieces of paper, because it will all be in one place in your book.

Make sure you carry the book around with you so that when people ask you to do something, you can write it down immediately in your book. Not only will this look impressive, but it will also ensure that you don't forget what you have been asked to do.

It will also help to eliminate interruptions. People will have seen you write things down and will therefore assume that you don't need to be reminded.

BRING FORWARD SYSTEM

A bring forward system is a concertina file, or drawer with lateral filing sections, numbered 1–31 (ie, representing the days in the month).

You put in it any written material that you need to see appear on your desk on any given day. For example, you sent a letter to someone on the 10th and you want to check that you have received a reply by the 25th. You would therefore put a copy of your letter in the slot marked 25. Every day you pull out all of the paper in the slot for that particular day (eg, everything in slot 25 on the 25th). Remove all the ones for action in the current month and put the others back until the next month.

ADVANTAGES OF A BRING FORWARD SYSTEM

- your desk should never be overflowing
- your pending action is all part processed
- nothing will appear at the last moment
- peaks and troughs will all be ironed out

TIME TO THINK PERIODS

A time to think period is the equivalent to having an office door which when closed means 'do not disturb' and when open means 'come in and chat'.

There will be two things that make having uninterrupted time difficult to achieve.

- you don't have an office – it's open plan
- you have to be available to people.

OPEN PLAN OFFICES

If you work in an open plan office, approach your colleagues and ask them if they would like two hours completely uninterrupted each week. The answer is almost undoubtedly going to be 'yes'. Make it a reciprocal arrangement. You answer each other's calls and deal with whatever can be dealt with for the other person for an agreed period of time. They do the same for you. You can come to this arrangement with members of your own team or with other people.

To make it work, make sure that you don't allow the other person to be interrupted and make it the same period of time every week. If you are going to permanently 'close' a section of your diary every week you should have some time, again specifically allocated, that is 'interruptible'.

You must also accept the fact that you are not indispensable. In fact, if no one can do your job when you are away, then you are unlikely to get any promotion. People will tend to interrupt you less if you tell them in advance when you are and aren't available. Say something like 'I'm always tied up on Wednesday mornings, but Wednesday afternoons is a good time to pop in and see me'.

You don't know who will turn up on Wednesday, but you can guarantee that someone probably will and plan your workload accordingly.

DEALING WITH TELEPHONE INTERRUPTIONS

Make telephone appointments. If you plan to ring someone, tell them (or whoever takes the message) the

EXAMPLE

TELEPHONE MESSAGE

TO: TIME:

FROM: DATE:

COMPANY: TAKEN BY:

TELEPHONE NO:

MESSAGE:

Please ring ☐   **Returned** ☐   **URGENT** ☐   **When**
back   **your call**   **available . . .**

specific time you will be calling. If you get a message that says that someone will call you 'sometime this afternoon', you will just carry on as normal. You may go into other people's offices, pop to the photocopier and so on. The chances are that when the person rings you will be away from your desk. If, however, you leave a message saying that Mavis Jones will be ringing you at 3pm then you are much more likely to be at your desk at that time.

- If you are asking someone to call you back, give them a specific time to call at. They are then more likely to return your call when it's convenient for you. They are also more likely to actually return your call.

- Learn the facilities that your telephone has to offer. Modern telephones have lots of facilities to help you to make better and more effective use of the telephone.

- If you telephone someone and they're unavailable, retain control of your time. Offer to ring *them* back at a specific time. This way you control when you interrupt your work and not the other person.

- Use telephone message forms and encourage the people you work with to do the same. If people are required to fill in specific forms, the questions on the form will prompt them to take the message down correctly.

MOVEMENT SHEETS

If you or your team spend time out of the office, produce weekly movement sheets. Keep a copy in the office and give copies to travelling staff. This saves time for people who ring the office only to find that a colleague is out for the day. It also looks more professional if a customer calls and you can simply look at a movement sheet and say where the individual is and when they are likely to be back in the office.

DEALING WITH INTERRUPTIONS

- Tell people in advance when you are and are not available and stick to it.

- When people do interrupt, tell them that you can't deal with them right now. Give them the reason (eg, you have to get a report done by 1200) and offer them an alternative time when you will be available to deal with them. People will respond positively if they feel you have taken their interruption seriously enough to offer them an alternative time.

- Stand up when people 'pop in' to discourage them from hanging around.

- Ask colleagues to put a call through to you when a perpetual interrupter turns up. The interrupter, seeing that you are busy may then go away.

- Pick up some papers from your desk and head towards the photocopier or the fax. This sometimes gives them the hint.

- Indicate at the beginning of the interruption that you only have a certain amount of time available to speak to the person. Say something like 'I've only got 10 minutes to talk to you Mike. I have to telephone Roberta at 3.30'.

- Don't be guilty of interrupting people yourself. Find out in advance when they are free and check out with them that it will be OK for you to pop in to see them.

HANDLING PAPERWORK

- Deal with paperwork at the same time each day, preferably first thing.

- Don't skim through it. Deal with each piece of paper as you pick it up.

- If you can action the document – do it. Then file the paper or throw it away.

- Begin action on anything that you can. Then file the document in the Bring Forward system for when you can take the next action.

- Read short items immediately (ie no longer than two sides of A4).

- Plan time to read longer documents.

- Pass along circulation items within 24 hours

- Don't file pieces of paper for the sake of it. Throw away anything that you don't actually need to be working on.

IN/ACTION/OUT TRAYS

You should only have two trays on your desk. One should be your in tray which you empty twice a day. The other

should be your filing tray which you empty at least once a day. Any items that are pending or you are working on should go into the Bring Forward system. This relieves the clutter on your desk.

Encourage people to put paperwork into your in tray. If your in tray is overflowing they will be reluctant to use it because they won't feel confident that you have seen the piece of paper. This is why you often find people put paper/correspondence right in the middle of your desk. If, however, they can see that you empty your in tray twice a day, they will at least feel confident that you have seen the piece of work that they have given you.

SUMMARY

- know how much time you spend on reactive and proactive tasks
- identify your job objectives and your priorities
- plan tasks in to your diary
- don't agree to unrealistic deadlines. Say 'No' and offer an alternative
- implement a rolling 'to do' list
- use an everything book for everything
- implement a bring forward system
- introduce 'Time to Think' periods to your colleagues
- make telephone appointments
- use movement sheets
- deal with each piece of paper only once
- only have two trays — in and out.

MANAGING STRESS

You often hear of 'executive' or 'managerial' stress but how often do people discuss 'administrative' or 'secretarial' stress?

Increasingly you are called on to deal with stressful situations at work and are often judged on how you perform on these occasions. This chapter is about learning to deal with personal stress in order to keep things in perspective when the pressures are piling up.

This concentrates on three main areas:

- what is stress?
- recognising stress and how it affects us
- how to deal with stress.

WHAT IS STRESS?

Is stress:

- positive or negative?
- a warning signal or a motivator?
- a handicap or a normal part of everyday life?

Stress is an inescapable part of modern life and it is no wonder that sometimes the twentieth century is referred to as the 'Aspirin Age'. Everyone seems to rush and hurry, with deadlines to meet and targets to achieve yesterday.

What sort of image does the word 'stress' conjure up in your mind? Is it one of distress or excitement; does it stretch you beyond endurance or give you that extra boost to reach your next hurdle?

The word 'stress' means many different things to different people and has been overloaded with meanings which were not in its original use. The word ' stress' has derived from the Latin Stringere meaning to 'pull tight'. In the seventeenth century it was associated with hardship and distress and in the eighteenth and nineteenth century with physics and engineering. Metallurgists, for example, test aircraft to see how much stress the metal can withstand before cracking or breaking up. If you imagine your body being put through a stress test, how often do you feel as if you are being 'pulled tight'?

People are all different and it is important to remember that what means stress to one person could mean excitement to another. One man's meat, is another man's poison!

Stress is about pressure and the reaction it produces within you. It can be brought about by external or internal factors. Often the internal factors are harder to deal with as you don't always recognise the pressure you put on yourself – it is much easier to blame someone or something else!

Cary Cooper's definition of stress is: 'An imbalance between the demand on a person and his or her ability to cope'!

It is your own personality and vulnerability to stress which you will often overlook.

Stress is the physiological and psychological reaction that occurs when people perceive an imbalance between the level of demand placed upon them and their capability for meeting that demand.

Today the term stress is almost like an umbrella under which anything goes when it describes a feeling of being pushed or pulled, squeezed or stretched. You need to recognise what stress is and what causes it and only then can you learn how to deal with it.

RECOGNISING STRESS AND HOW IT AFFECTS US

In order to be honest with yourself and recognise the pressures, you need to get away from the taboo of stress. Stress is normal and indeed with no stress at all we would be dead! Stress is a very individual thing and everyone has very different stress levels.

Successful stress management requires you to recognise when you are experiencing stress, whether positive or negative, as it can indeed be either beneficial or destructive.

Everyone needs a certain level of pressure to perform but how far do you push? We are a little like a set of scales with stressors being the various weights placed upon us. The piece of work with 'urgent – needed yesterday' waiting on your desk amidst a pile of other messages and deadlines can be the large potato which tips the scales. You need to recognise your optimum levels and when you tip

one way or the other. You often hear of the term 'burn-out' when too much has been placed on our scales over a period of time. However on the other side there is 'rust out' when there is not enough stress to motivate you. Both underload and overload can have an equally debilitating effect on your performance at work and is illustrated in the following diagram. It is impossible to always stay at the optimum level but with good stress management techniques you can maintain a balance. If under loaded, as stimulus increases so does performance, but if pushed over the top then performance will drop, often leading to exhaustion and illness.

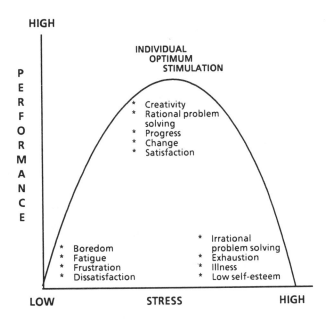

From: Beyond Stress to Effective Management
By: Walter H. Gmelch

Bodies can normally be quite strong and flexible. However you are a little like elastic – it springs back into shape but if stressed too much for too long it can lose its elasticity for good. This is why it is so essential to recognise the warning signs of excessive stress.

When you are under stress you may have physical as well as emotional reactions which then can affect your behaviour. You invariably start seeing yourself and your world in a different and more negative way. These physical, emotional and behavioural changes are normally your body trying to tell you your stress levels are higher than they should be. If you start recognising your own personal signs they can act as a very useful early warning system!

Listed below are some of the most common signs. You may have others of your own.

PHYSICAL	EMOTIONAL
Appetite – Increase or decrease	Sense of failure
Sleep – Increase or decrease	Tearful
Breathlessness	Loss of confidence
Hot/Cold	Isolated
Dry mouth	Withdrawn
Trembling	Low self-esteem
Nervous twitches	Clumsy
Nausea	Irrational
Muscular tension	Inability to concentrate
Headaches	Loss of interest

Low self esteem is a very common reaction to stress and this changes your feeling about yourself and the way you react to the world. Other feelings may be:

- ugly

- clumsy

- overwhelmed

- guilty

- angry

- less competent

Sometimes you become totally irrational and no amount of reassurance, positive feedback or irrefutable evidence to the contrary will convince you that you are OK!

The following questionnaire highlights some common reactions to stress and may help you to recognise when your body is telling you to slow down. Do not panic (or feel stressed!) if you answer yes to many of them as they are very common reactions to pressure.

You may respond differently in very similar situations however you may be able to identify certain typical responses to set the alarm bells ringing.

DO YOU RECOGNISE WHEN YOUR BODY IS TELLING YOU THAT YOU ARE UNDER STRESS?

Read each of the statements below and tick any that apply to you when you are under pressure:

1. I am easily irritated. ☐
2. I have difficulty concentrating for any length of time. ☐
3. I feel tired even when I wake up in the morning. ☐
4. I have difficulty making even simple decisions. ☐
5. The quality of my sleep has deteriorated. I have difficulty getting to sleep and/or I wake during the night and am restless. ☐
6. I lose my temper frequently. ☐
7. I feel powerful negative emotions. ☐
8. I feel generally run down and rather unwell. ☐
9. Life seems to be quite hopeless. Nothing seems worthwhile and I feel really low. ☐
10. My eating pattern has altered. I have lost my

appetite or I seem to be eating more food to
comfort myself. ☐
11. I have difficulty in absorbing new data. ☐
12. I suffer from frequent headaches. ☐
13. I have difficulty recalling information when I am
required to do so. ☐
14. I am drinking more alcohol than usual. ☐
15. I experience dramatic swings of mood. ☐
16. I have missed, or been late for, one or two
important appointments. ☐
17. I feel wound up and unable to relax properly. ☐
18. I am unable to achieve my normal level of
creativity. ☐
19. I suffer from backache regularly. ☐
20. I feel inadequate and unable to cope. ☐
21. I have taken time off work. ☐
22. I suffer from indigestion. ☐
23. I seem to lack the capacity to focus on a particular
problem – my mind keeps wandering on to other
issues. ☐
24. The least little thing sends me into a panic. ☐
25. I smoke more cigarettes than usual. ☐
26. I have a frequent need to urinate. ☐
27. In discussion with other people I constantly repeat
myself. ☐
28. My driving is rather erratic and my judgement
impaired. ☐
29. I seem to spend all my time worrying. ☐
30. I feel very lethargic and disinterested with work
and/or life. ☐

COPING WITH STRESS

There are five main ways of coping with stress:

- understanding and acceptance of self

- tackling the problem

- self nurturing

- emotional expression

- active distraction.

UNDERSTANDING AND ACCEPTANCE OF SELF

In order to be able to cope with stress you need to:

- understand your needs and motives

- know your own values and priorities

- accept yourself and your limitations

- recognise your stressors.

Be honest with yourself and look at where your demands come from. You will place much higher demands on yourself than others do, but you may still blame everyone else for your stress!

Often the standards you set yourself are irrational and unrealistic. . . 'Everyone must like me'. . . 'I should be a perfect wife, mother, housekeeper AND employee!'

TRYING TO BE PERFECT LEADS TO BURNOUT

When you are under stress you often add to it by trying to be everything to everybody. You become so busy being so busy that you don't leave time to think about yourself and why you are experiencing pressure.

Identify and clarify your own values and priorities. If you are not clear on what is valuable to you you will seesaw depending on everyone else's expectations and demands.

Write down your own values and expectations. This will help you to set limits and boundaries.

When experiencing stress and pressure instead of immediately looking to cast the blame on an external factor look to yourself and see what is going on inside!

Dealing with stress means understanding yourself. It is not just about coping with the world around you, but learning to cope with the world within you.

An American poet, Henry Longfellow sums it up in the following words:

'Not in the clamour of the crowded street, Not in the shouts and plaudits of the throng, but in ourselves, are triumph and defeat'.

TACKLING THE PROBLEM

Once you have identified what is causing you stress you need to look at what you can do about it. Often you may spend time worrying about a situation but not actually doing anything. 90% of that time is worrying about things that never happen and as Winston Churchill said: 'There's a lot of trouble in life, most of which has not happened'.

Take action over the things that are really worrying you. If you can't take action then learn to let go. After all, worrying is like a rocking chair; it gives you something to do but gets you nowhere!

Tackling a problem means first identifying what it is and then starting the 'tackling process'.

The 'tackling process' means you:

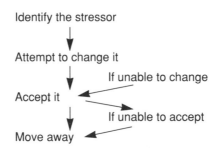

Worrying is a waste of valuable time and effort if there is nothing you can do to change the situation. By 'letting go' you can channel your energies into more productive areas.

The following prayer sums up the key to tackling problems:

> 'God please grant me the serenity
> to accept things I can not change
> The courage to change the things I can
> And the wisdom to know the difference!'

Look at your list of stressors NOW and identify those which you can take action on and give yourself realistic deadlines.

Problem/Stressor	Proposed Action	When

SELF-NURTURING

When you are suffering from stress you need to pay extra attention to yourself and look after your body and mind. However what often happens is you tend to forget your own needs; develop low self-esteem and generally add to your feeling of self-worthlessness.

Think of your body as if it was a car: Stress is like the choke – a little is good for you and gives your body the kick-start it might need to operate. However if you leave the choke out all day it damages the engine and raises the fuel consumption. If your car starts to back-fire or the engine starts to splutter, would you drive it faster? If there is dirt in the carburettor or the petrol is running low, do you fill up with diesel instead of four-star? I am sure you would take it to the garage for a service or to have it checked and refuelled. This is how you should treat your body.

During times of extreme stress your self-image will tend to drop and this will add to your feeling of negativity. The first step in self-nurturing is to boost your self-image. Then look after your body.

SELF-IMAGE BOOST! . . .

- accept compliments (don't deny them)
- acknowledge your value (write a list of things you are good at)
- praise yourself when you do well
- work at having pleasure without guilt
- treat yourself as you would like others to treat you
- treat your body well – it is the only one you have got.

- Learn to like yourself (after all you want others to like you).

- Write a list of things you like about YOU (if you find this hard — ask a friend).

You need to take care of yourself and your body. If you feel the pressures are building up then give yourself a treat. This does not need to mean expense! If your stressor is an overdraft or a financial crisis don't add to it by treating yourself to something expensive from Harrods! A treat could be something as simple as taking the scenic route home; ringing an old friend you haven't spoken to for a while; a long soak in the bath or taking the time to admire something beautiful!

When you wake up feeling stressed and wishing the whole world would go away it is easy to take that feeling with you throughout the whole day and go to bed that evening feeling even worse. Self-nurturing means working on yourself and convincing your body that you are OK. If you feel stressed you will tend to tell yourself you feel awful and act accordingly. Behave and act as if you are feeling great and you'll be surprised how quickly you start to actually believe it! Instead of getting up in slow-motion speed up.

It is up to you whether you dance around the house with music on or put on news that is depressing and listen to your own negative thoughts on life. It is important to realise that you can change your point of view and therefore your feelings by the way you treat yourself. TREAT YOURSELF AS YOU WOULD LIKE THE WORLD TO TREAT YOU!

EMOTIONAL EXPRESSION

When suffering from stress one of the common reactions is to because withdrawn and to feel isolated. At a time when you most need to express your feelings you will often hold them in and become more 'alone'.

Your body's health can be a reflection of your mental health and physical illness can often be a result of unresolved inner conflicts. If you are experiencing feelings of panic, fear, threat or pressure you need to let those feelings out and express them. Repressed feelings and emotions can affect your health both mentally and physically. How often do you sit with a smile on your face and stew inside? To be healthy and energetic you need to maintain positive emotions and not let the negative ones take over. In order to do this you need to be expressing your feelings.

YOU NEED TO ACCEPT YOURSELF AND LOVE YOURSELF WHERE YOU ARE RIGHT NOW!

Take action by:

- Developing a support network

- Having regular two-way communication (particularly with your boss!)

- Accepting that emotions are OK

- Accepting your own feelings -
  Let them out, don't deny them

- Sharing your feelings with someone you trust.

One very good way of letting go of emotions is by using the powerful natural tool of laughter. A university in America did a three year study on laughter. The only evolutionary purpose of laughter that they could find was to relieve stress! Under stress you may lose your sense of humour and not feel able to laugh.

When sitting at your desk with deadlines to meet and pressures piling up you can easily become so bogged down with the problems that *you* become the problem. If you can maintain a perspective you can look at the problem from the outside rather than from the confused middle.

Problems are often serious. However they are not going to be solved by walking around with a serious face. Keep a small sign above your desk which reads:

TAKE YOURSELF LIGHTLY AND YOUR JOB SERIOUSLY!

If you are feeling as if you should have been born an octopus and that there are not enough hours in the day – instead of sitting and telling yourself that you are under stress, you need to lighten up. When you tell yourself that you are under pressure your body believes you and tenses up. The pressure is then increased as you develop a headache or get tense muscles which ache and remind your brain that you are stressed. Break the cycle by learning to relax.

When you laugh your body relaxes and in turn your brain will feel more relaxed and be able to tackle those problems in a refreshed manner.

To help you smile (and I do not mean a fixed grin that makes you look as if you have slept with a coat hanger in your mouth!!) which will make you relax, you can;

- Keep a few funny pictures in your desk that you can take out and look at.

- Remember an embarrassing moment.

- Think of a funny story or joke (or person!).

- Take a mini-vacation (Shut your eyes for a few moments and take yourself to a place where you feel peaceful).

- Remember that you are not the centre of the universe and it really is not the end of the world.

The key to emotional expression is to let those feelings out in the air and is summed up in this Tibetan proverb:

'HOLD IT IN ALL YOU LIKE –
IT WILL NOT GO AWAY UNTIL YOU LET IT OUT'.

ACTIVE DISTRACTION

Active distraction means being able to switch off and re-charge your stressed batteries so that your body is not under constant pressure. Many people find this the most difficult thing to do as they just keep busy so that they don't have to think about the problem.

You will often get so wrapped up in the pressures that you will be unable to think of anything else. You spend so much time worrying and cursing the problem that you are unable to switch off. Using active distraction is a way of enabling you to divert your mind away from your problems. That way you refresh your mind and body and are able to tackle the problem with renewed vigour.

> 'IT IS BETTER TO LIGHT A CANDLE THAN
> TO CURSE THE DARKNESS' Chinese proverb.

It is important that you are able to:

- Draw the line

- Mark the end of the day by leaving work behind

At work you need to have distractions as well. How often when you are busy do you miss your coffee or lunch breaks?

At work active distractions can be:

- A mini-vacation.

- Coffee break.

- A stress toy.

- Relaxing your body by tensing and releasing.

- Scrunch toes tight and then relax whilst imagining all the stress flowing from each toe as you release and relax.

- Relax your mind by thinking of something funny or different.

- Keep a perspective on your problem.

In caring for yourself it is important to:

- Take time out: 'ME' time which is for you!

- Exercise

- Relax

SUMMARY

- Identify your stress factors.

- Remember that different people deal with stress differently.

- Recognise your own personal symptoms of stress.

- Accept yourself.

- Tackle the problem.

- Nurture yourself.

Cartoons in this chapter by Theresa Lemonde

PROJECT ADMINISTRATION

You have just been told you are to be a member of a team to carry out a project over the next five months. The project leader and other members of the team are from different departments. You have never been involved in any projects before so you still feel confused, although flattered to be selected. You know there are others in the organisaiton who have had project experience and you are concerned that your own knowledge and skills are not sufficient for the role. In addition you already have a full daily work load so you can not see how you can take on additional responsibilities unless there are some changes in the department.

This chapter aims to help you understand what a project involves and suggests some of the things you can do to make an effective contribution to the project team and achieve success.

WHAT IS A PROJECT?

A simple definition is:

> *Any group of tasks that must be completed in a specified time period, often with specified cost constraints, using the most appropriate people in the organisation.*

The time period may be a few weeks to several months or even longer, depending on the type of project. The costs of project work are often not measured apart from capital expenditure, such as new equipment. This is because your time is divided between your day-to-day operational duties and the tasks assigned to you for the project. The cost of your time is then regarded as an overhead within your department's operating budget. However, as more organisations realise the importance of projects, time is measured and costed as a way of improving project effectiveness.

The most important characteristic is clearly the deadline for completion. After all, you would be most upset if your travel agent failed to issue your airline tickets for your holiday to enable you to get on the flight! The results of any project are needed by the business by a specified date for carefully selected reasons. Failure to provide the results means possible financial loss for the organisation or other serious implications.

Projects can be regarded as *special* tasks that are important to the organisation and must be completed on time. So as a participating team member, you must be prepared to complete your contribution to the results within the agreed timetable. It is clearly important for you to have the right skills for the work assigned to you. Many projects are perceived to fail because the right people, with appropriate skills are not included in the project team. Team membership must not be based on just availability, popularity and present workload.

TYPES OF PROJECTS

Some examples are:

- designing and implementing new procedures
- launching a new product
- an office re-organisation or move
- developing a new service
- setting up a sales campaign
- market research
- production cost savings.

All involve change, so you can also define a project as:

a means of successfully achieving a significant change in the business

Most projects involve some input from several departments at some time in the project life. It is the management of the people in these different locations in your organisation that leads to the essential elements of the role of **Project Leader**. Control of the project is a dynamic process requiring the use of many skills to achieve the desired results, a process recognised today as **Project Management**.

THE PROJECT PROCESS

All projects have a finite life cycle, usually recognised as *four phases*:

- conception
- planning
- start-up and execution
- run down and termination.

Each of these phases can be clearly defined and the Project Leader has specific actions to carry out in each, if the project is to achieve the desired results. Effective team working is essential to enable this success and you must pay particular attention to supporting teamwork through:

- communicating openly with all the team members and the leader
- willingly offering your ideas and suggestions
- participating positively in team meetings
- demonstrating your commitment to the project

- accepting agreed targets for your contribution

- agreeing priorities for your project work (over other duties)

- completing your assigned work on time

- anticipating, identifying and exposing problems

- contributing to problem solving.

Everything you do in the project is derived from your concern for the project and its results, not satisfying your personal ego. Apart from your general contribution to teamwork, there are specific actions you must take in each of the four phases.

PHASE 1 – CONCEPTION

At the start of the project process the *objectives* must be clearly defined – often a difficult thing to do. This requires the team to clearly state the problem or need and identify the purpose of seeking a solution. This helps to identify the potential benefits and leads to deriving the actual results the organisation needs to achieve with the deadlines for completion. These statements together, termed the *Objective Statement* must then be agreed with the *Project Sponsor* (or Senior Management). During this phase you can:

- identify all the people you believe have an interest in the project – both during the project and after completion

- ensure you clearly understand the problem or need and the purpose of the project. If you do not then ASK QUESTIONS NOW

- tell your project leader if you believe the results

required are unreal or not achievable, giving reasons why. This must be resolved before entering Phase 2

- expose any past experience you have of similar problems that may have relevance

- identify any special Company standards or specifications you believe are relevant to the project.

The project process is based on taking a logical approach to the work. Do NOT attempt to jump in half way through or do things the leader has not asked you to do. Attempting to derive a project plan with incomplete information will surely lead to failure and all your efforts are then completely wasted.

I'M STILL NOT CLEAR, EITHER. BUT THE MAIN THRUST IS OBVIOUSLY TO MAKE A DRAMATIC INCREASE IN OUR USE OF FLIPCHARTS

PHASE 2 – PLANNING

This phase involves everyone in the project team asking some simple questions:

1 What have we done before?

2 What do we need to do now?

3 What do we NOT need to do?

4 How long is each part of the work going to take?

The most effective way to answer these questions is to hold a brainstorming session. Use a flip chart and note down ALL the ideas and tasks identified. Then group the obviously related tasks together in clusters. Each of these clusters are the principle *activities* of the project, often termed the *key stages* and are used to derive the *base plan*. You must then decide how these activities relate to each other through their inter-dependencies and this is done by a process of **taskboarding**. Write each activity on a self-adhesive notelet or file-card and then as a team activity agree the logical order and relationships between all the activities. To derive the *dependency* between activities ask:

1 What can we do next?

2 What must have been completed before we can start the next activity.

Place the notelets on a flip chart sheet or white-board in the agreed order working from the project start on the left to the project end on the right side. Show the *dependency links* by drawing arrows between the related activities to give you the *logic diagram*. An example is shown in Figure 9.1.

Clearly label each activity with a code number and then decide how long each is likely to take to complete. This is where the planning process can get complex and one way to resolve the time issue is for each member of the

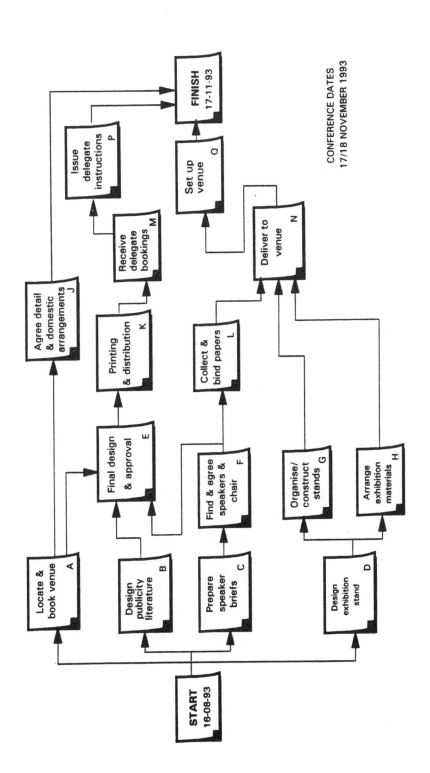

Figure 9.1 *Logic diagram for organising a conference*

CONFERENCE DATES
17/18 NOVEMBER 1993

133

team is to determine their capacity to carry out their part of the project work:

1 Initially decide how long it would take you to complete the work if you had nothing else to do, working continuously on the project.

2 Write down a list of all the other things you know you have to do each week as part of your job, including attending meetings and then assign a time in hours to each task on this list.

3 To allow for interruptions, chasing other people and information, fire-fighting, unforeseen events and external commitments, reduce your official working week hours by 20%. e.g. a 40 hour week reduces to an 'effective' week of 32 hours. This is then a more realistic assessment of your 'productive' time at work.

4 Subtract the total derived in 2 above from the productive week derived in 3 above. The difference, if you have any time left, is the *capacity* you have for the project work.

5 Apply your capacity factor to the project times you decided in 1 above to get a realistic time for your project work to be completed.

The problem with time allocation to the plan is that you probably have little or no spare time, i.e. your *capacity factor* is close to zero! Even if you have a reasonable capacity, the real time to complete the work may be unacceptable to the project leader. As project work is nearly always really 'extra work' you are now faced with a problem – how to take on the project work and still fulfil your other obligations. You have several options available to you:

- Review your operational duties you listed earlier and the time each takes to carry out. Can you reduce your estimates realistically? Most people tend to under-estimate so do not fool yourself!

- Can you reduce your operational workload by sharing some of your duties with other colleagues or junior staff in your department?

- Discuss the situation with your manager, who should be aware of the priority status of the project. The priority of your normal workload can then be assessed and decisions made about reallocating responsibilities to other member of the department.

- Reduce your contribution to the project, suggesting someone else should join the team.

This process requires effort and commitment to derive realistic project activity times that are acceptable to all those involved and it must be applied rigorously to every activity in the project. It is *critical to achieving success* in the project.

When all the project times are derived they can be entered into the base plan and presented in a format that is easily understood by everyone – the *bar chart*. This is the most common working document that displays the project plan in a graphic form which is used for controlling the project by regular updating to show the project status at any point in time. An example bar chart is shown in Figure 9.2.

Finally having agreed your contribution to the project, both as tasks and time to complete each, you need to derive a *work plan* for your actual work. Since the original activities in the plan actually comprise a cluster of separate tasks you must identify these, list them and fit them within the limits of time agreed. A typical example is shown in Figure 9.3. Each task is listed with an estimate of the time required, remembering to use consistent time units

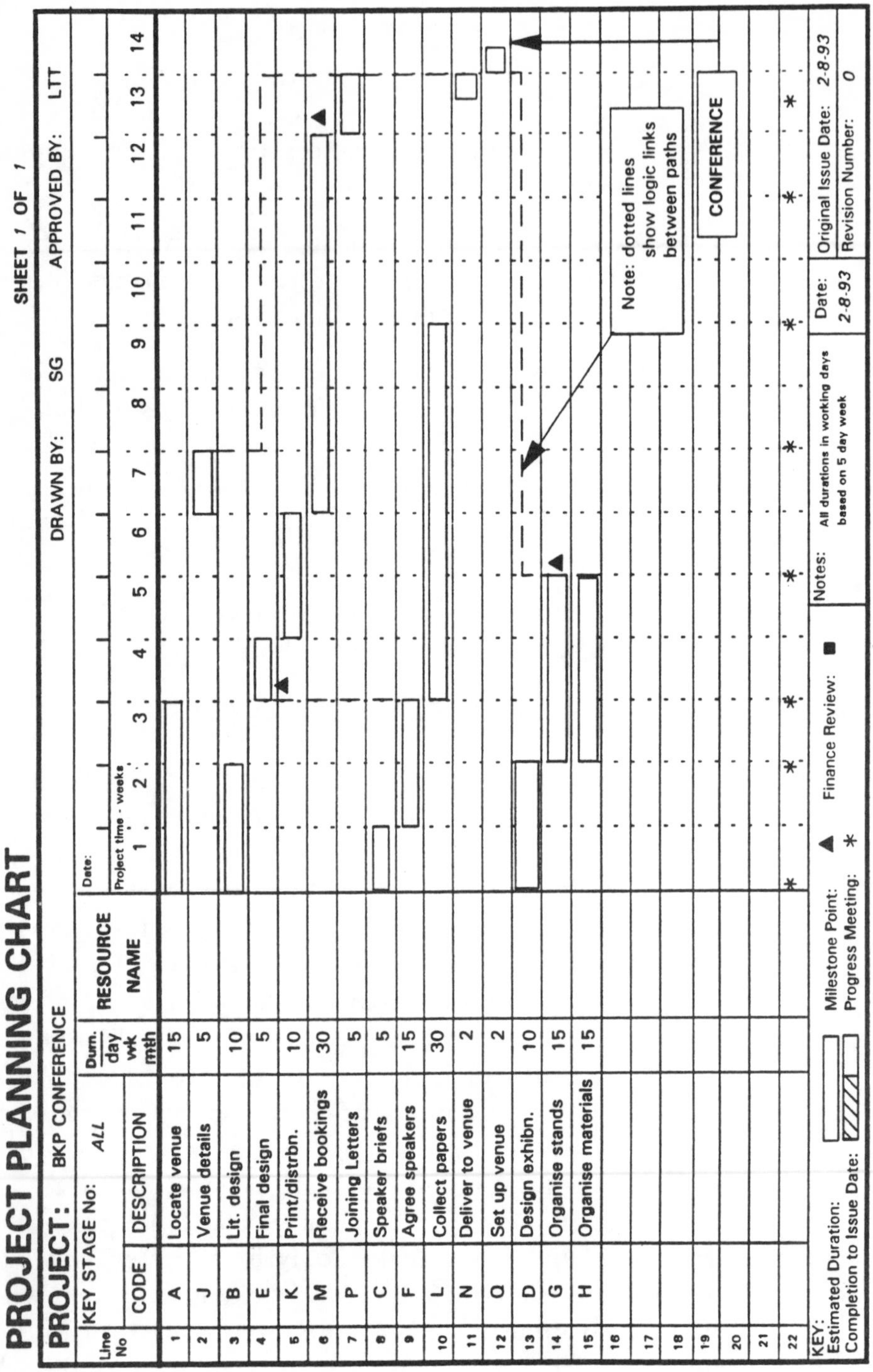

PROJECT PLANNING CHART

SHEET 1 OF 1

PROJECT: BKP CONFERENCE

DRAWN BY: SG   APPROVED BY: LTT

Line No	KEY STAGE No: ALL		RESOURCE	Dur. day wk mth	Project time - weeks
	CODE	DESCRIPTION	NAME		1 2 3 4 5 6 7 8 9 10 11 12 13 14
1	A	Locate venue		15	
2	J	Venue details		5	
3	B	Lit. design		10	
4	E	Final design		5	
5	K	Print/distrbn.		10	
6	M	Receive bookings		30	
7	P	Joining Letters		5	
8	C	Speaker briefs		5	
9	F	Agree speakers		15	
10	L	Collect papers		30	
11	N	Deliver to venue		2	
12	Q	Set up venue		2	
13	D	Design exhibn.		10	
14	G	Organise stands		15	
15	H	Organise materials		15	
16					
17					
18					
19					CONFERENCE
20					
21					
22					

Note: dotted lines show logic links between paths

KEY:
Estimated Duration: ▭
Completion to Issue Date: ▨

Milestone Point: ■
Progress Meeting: ▭

Finance Review: ◀
*

Notes: All durations in working days based on 5 day week

Date: 2-8-93
Original Issue Date: 2-8-93
Revision Number: 0

Figure 9.2 *A project planning bar chart*

WORK PLAN RECORD

| Key Stage No: | B – LITERATURE | Sponsor: L. T. THOMPSON |
| Work Plan Code: | BKP/B/06/- | Project Leader: S. GLOVER |
| PROJECT: BKP CONFERENCE |
Scheduled Start Date:	16.08.93	Issued To: JOHN LEVER	Account No:
Scheduled Finish Date:	27.08.93	Department: MARKETING	Budget Centre:
Scheduled Duration:	10 Days / Weeks / Months		Sheet No.: 1 of 1

KEY STAGE SCHEDULE
Units: 0.5D per column

Line No.	Code	ACTIVITIES	COMMENTS	Line No.
1	01	PREPARE OUTLINE COPY		1
2	02	PREPARE BROCHURE LAYOUT		2
3	03	SUBMIT COPY/LAYOUT FOR APPROVAL	(S.GLOVER/F.JESSOP)	3
4	04	REVISE COPY/LAYOUT		4
5	05	PREPARE BOOKING FORM		5
6	06	IDENTIFY MAILING LIST		6
7	07	PREPARE DATABASE FOR LABELS	(INFORM LYNN)	7
8	08	GET PRINTING QUOTES		8
9	09	BOOK TEMP STAFF FOR STUFFING		9
10				10
11				11
12				12

ISSUE DATE: 11-08-93	Inform progress:	S. GLOVER
	Available for advice:	F. JESSOP
	Consult for problems:	S. GLOVER

| Schedule agreed: | .... | Operator |
| Schedule approved: | .... | Project Leader |

Figure 9.3 *Work Plan Record – an example*

137

throughout. Then mark in the times for each on the bar chart section of the work plan using a 'trough' symbol for each. Get the final activity work plan approved by the project leader and your manager and then you are ready to start work.

PHASE 3 – START-UP AND EXECUTION

The final step in the planning process links to project start-up. The project leader must establish the project administration and procedures that the team must follow for project control. Frequently this involves setting up specific procedures for reporting progress of the work and taking appropriate actions when things start to go wrong. Control involves measuring variances from the base plan and reacting with corrective actions. Failure to do this will court potential failure of the project!

It is a common complaint that no-one is sure whether the project has actually started or who is doing what and who has specific responsibilities. With any project there is clearly a need to ensure everyone understands their role and this is easily achieved by holding a project launch meeting. This formal gathering of the project team with the sponsor or senior management gives the project leader an opportunity to explain the base plan and everyone's responsibilities under that plan. The meeting allows people to feel part of the team with a sense of ownership of the project objectives and build commitment to achieve a successful outcome. The occasion can be made even more valuable by adding a social element such as refreshments and a buffet lunch.

The execution of the project requires everyone involved to fulfil their agreed commitments on time and participate in effective working of the team. As a participating team member you can contribute to this teamwork if you:

- Make regular status reports on your work to the project leader.

- Report verbally to the project leader regularly.

- Anticipate potential risks and problems and react to these.

- Keep your project leader and manager informed if problems occur.

- Have regular 1:1 meetings with your manager to ensure you keep a balance between your project work and operational responsibilities.

- Attend the 1:1 meetings arranged by your project leader.

- Identify any skills shortcomings you feel may be slowing down your project work — seek guidance and help from the project leader.

- Attend project team meetings and briefings on time and contribute constructively to discussions. Keep your status reports accurate, brief and clear.

- Co-operate with other team members seeking your assistance — you may need help from them later.

- Maintain close attention to the quality of your work — do not be satisfied with second best.

- Take care not to deviate from the agreed plan. If you have some new ideas, tell the project leader. A decision can then be made to change the plan if appropriate.

- If your operational duties change due to unforeseen events, inform the project leader immediately that your project schedule is vulnerable and delays may occur. Appropriate action can then be agreed.

- If the project objectives change, then accept the decision and contribute willingly to any need to replan, even if this means redoing or duplicating work completed. Identify the impact of the change on both your project work and operational duties.

- If you are asked to provide a record of your time keep a daily time sheet of how you spend your time.

- Take care not to incur additional, unscheduled time for yourself or others without informing your project leader. If project costs are recorded and monitored the project leader may need to adjust the budget.

- Evaluate your own performance frequently – always ask yourself if you can improve the way you carry out your responsibilities. Set yourself targets to improve performance and discuss these with your project leader and manager. Seek help if appropriate.

- Identify opportunities for further training you feel could help your development.

- Learn from the successes as well as the failures. If your time estimates turn out to be misconceived, ask yourself why and note what you can do to avoid the error in future. If problems occur, learn from how they are solved to anticipate or avoid them in future.

- Participate constructively in problem solving sessions with the team.

- Organise yourself:

  – maintain tidy paperwork records

    – keep project records in special files

    – retain copies of reports issued

    – record accurate notes yourself in all meetings

    – keep a project log book.

The project leader is accountable to the sponsor for the delivery of the project objectives in accordance with the agreed schedule. This can not be achieved without a high level of concern for effective communication in the team to ensure everyone involved participates fully and fulfils their responsibilities. Your contribution, like everyone in the team is critical to this success and it is your obligation to pay particular attention to the above list of actions. Your manager expects you to complete your other operational work to accepted normal standards. Balancing these two requirements often leads to conflicts that can only be resolved by cool and constructive discussion. If you foresee any conflicts occurring, identify the potential problem with the project leader and your manager as they may have to meet to discuss a solution. Do not hope the conflict will just go away – it rarely does, and it is always better to plan ahead to avoid a problem rather than be forced into taking action in a damage limitation exercise later.

PHASE 4 – RUN-DOWN AND TERMINATION

As the project progresses towards completion the project leader will start to plan this phase in more detail. The run-down of a project involves the team in reviewing the objectives and the status of achievement of each. This leads to an assessment of any part of the work that might need to be repeated or revised within the existing schedule to ensure final success. During the lifetime of the project the business needs may have changed and possibly the results achieved are no longer needed in the same form or in their entirety. Adjustments have to be made to the remainder of the plan to take these changes into account.

In addition the team must now start to think about what happens when the project is finished. This often raises further difficulties because many projects never seem to finish! They just go on and on, adding refinements here, modifications there and even additional objectives. It may appear logical to do 'just a bit more work' while the team is working well together and before the team members get assigned to other work or projects. The temptation to introduce *project drift* is potentially dangerous. It can dramatically add to the overall project costs with the risk of limited results, poor control, lowering of morale, and cause a perception of failure in the eyes of the non-participants.

It is most important then, for the project to have a clearly defined *declared end date*. This does not prevent further *follow-on projects* to be established to look at the possible refinements, even with all or part of the same project team. These follow-on projects can be based on clear objectives to achieve specific results:

- to implement the project results

- to establish and carry out a training programme

- to extend the scope of the project

- to extend the application of the project results

- to establish and implement a maintenance and service programme

- to establish and implement a user help facility.

Unless these and similar areas of the project have been included in the original base plan, each of these must be treated as new projects and taken through the same project process steps as before.

The termination of the project involves the team in two specific groups of activities:

- project closure
- post-project evaluation and review.

The project closure is the formal end of the project where some clearly defined tasks must be carried out:

- the results are recorded and signed off as accepted by the sponsor
- reporting procedures are terminated in a final status report
- any outstanding contracts – both internal and external, are terminated
- the final cost of the project is calculated and budget variance recorded
- all project records are finally updated for archiving.

Project completion is a suitable occasion (hopefully) for celebration with a final project meeting staged in a similar way to the start-up or launch meeting. The results can be formally presented to senior management. Explaining how and why the results have turned out as seen and identifying the impact of these results on the business. As a project nears completion there is often a tendency for pressure to be applied to close the project prematurely with a provisional acceptance of the results. This should be avoided wherever possible. It can lead to implementation of the results in an incomplete manner, creating potential conflicts of interests, team fragmentation and demotivation.

The post project evaluation and review is the final activity for the project team before it is finally disbanded formally. Until this is complete no member of the team can regard the job as finished. Too often in practice, pressure of work is allowed to dictate priorities in a different direction, either for other projects or operational duties. The project review is essential to establish clearly that the project achieved its intended outcomes. But there is also another important aspect to this activity. It is the last opportunity the project team has to examine the project process in detail and evaluate how it was carried out in reality. The team needs to address many questions that can lead to improvements in the project process in the organisation and identify learning points for future projects. Some key questions you can ask are:

- Were the objectives correctly stated?

- Were all the objectives met?

- Are the objectives all still valid?

- Did the sponsor maintain active support for the project throughout?

- Was the leadership of the project effective throughout?

- Was the team membership appropriate?

- Was the project plan effective and accurate?

- Did you miss out important tasks initially?

- Was the team actively involved in planning?

- Could you have anticipated some of the problems you encountered?

- Did you deal with problems and conflicts promptly?

- Did you perform tasks on time to the schedules?

- Did your administration procedures work effectively?

- Was communication in the team good throughout?

There are many other questions you can ask and each of them leads you to ask consequential questions like 'If not, why not?' You can get the value from your experiences throughout the project by suggesting ways to improve the project process, both for yourself and others on future project teams.

The results of this review need to be put into a *final evaluation and review* report with clear recommendations from the evaluation process. This report must be available to all those people who can benefit from these learning points. If your organisation has established a **Project Process Manual** then the learning points can be incorporated into the established procedures. If no such manual exists, perhaps you can suggest now is the time to consider having one for the organisation.

THE PROJECT LOG BOOK

You can now appreciate that the management of projects is potentially a complex activity. This is compounded by the probability that you are not just working on one project at any time, but have obligations to contribute to two or even more teams made up of different people. This creates more difficulties in planning and organising your work load between projects and other duties. In assessing your workload at the planning stage of a new project, include commitments you have already for ongoing projects before taking on more work. Most people are over-optimistic in estimating how long a task will take and evaluation will help you to sharpen your estimating skills. There is no easy answer to estimating time to execute a task – it is based totally on your experience. No two people carry out the same task at the same pace, so estimates are personal to each individual.

An essential tool for your personal organisation where you can record project information is the **_project log book_**. This is preferably a hard bound A4 notebook where you make explicit notes about everything that happens during the project. Start a new page for each day and make notes on at least:

- Your time estimates and where they go wrong (and why).

- Records of ALL relevant telephone conversations.

- Commitments made in meetings with your manager.

- Commitments made in meetings with your project leader.

- What happens in project meetings.

- Actions you accept in project meetings.

- Records of meetings with other team members.

- Records of meetings with external suppliers, contractors etc.

- Learning points from problem solving sessions.

- Any reminders for yourself relevant to the project.

Keep the log book strictly for project notes ONLY and have a separate one for each project in which you are involved. You will find each will contain a wealth of useful information to refer to that can help you improve your performance in projects in future.

A FINAL NOTE

Success in project work requires a high level of commitment and dedication and sometimes a little luck helps! However getting the right results on time is always difficult with all the other pressures you face in your day to day activities. The foundations of success are built on good organisation and effective use of your time to give a quality performance at all times. If the team works well together, always bearing these factors in mind, then you will achieve satisfaction in your work and feel rewarded by the successful completion of the project.

FURTHER READING

In the Manager's Pocket Guide Series published by The Industrial Society:
- Leading Projects
- Planning Projects
- Implementing Projects

COPING WITH CHANGE

WHAT IS CHANGE?

The dictionary tells us that change means becoming different; moving from present to future or the difference between where we are nowand where we will be.

We all live and work in a changing environment and changes at work seem to be gathering pace.

Just think of the changes over the past 25 years:

- New technology – move from typewriters to WP
- Fax – enabling quicker movement of information
- E-Mail
- Flexitime working – giving staff freedom of choice
- Relocation of companies

What does the future hold?

- Teleworking from home
- Working in EEC – larger markets
- Video conferencing – saving travel time
- Job share or part-time working
- More career breaks – secondments; maternity leave
- More career moves – relocating
- Job changes to stay in work – learning new skills

Summary:

- Change has always been with us
- Changes at work will continue to affect us
- If we don't change we get left behind

WHAT CAUSES CHANGE?

Changes at work come about for a number of reasons:

- Economic necessity eg recession
- Legislation eg Health & Safety requirements
- Competition – keeping up to date
- Changing markets to meet customer needs
- Companies relocating to expand or reduce costs
- New technology – reducing/increasing staff
- New senior management styles
- Existing equipment no longer viable – too costly to repair.

Changes are often planned by senior management, usually 5-10 years ahead. Many organisations identify where they would like to be and produce a mission statement. They may then produce a business plan showing how they intend to get there. Other changes may need to happen almost overnight, depending on the causes.

e.g.   During the 1970's industrial action by the power workers brought about the urgent introduction of the three-day working week for many companies. This meant starting earlier and finishing later on those three days to cover for the loss of the other two days without power. This change in itself led to many organisations later introducing flexitime working for staff.

HOW DOES IT AFFECT YOU?

If change is inevitable why do people normally resist it?

When you decide personally to make a change in your life or at work – that decision is within your control. If you don't like it you can always change again. You decide what, when and how.

However, changes that affect you at work are usually outside your control. Someone else has made the decision, you usually hear about it from your manager.

If you are happy and comfortable with what you are currently doing even the smallest change will have some affect on you.

How do people normally react to change? –

- Resentment – 'change for change sake'

- Fear – can they cope with new role; new systems?

- Will they have a job?

- Will they like the new job; new system; new team?

- Anger and bewilderment – not understanding reasons behind change

- Sadness at loss of familiar things

- Hostility – 'it won't work'

- Stress and depression

- Loss of confidence

To have these feelings is perfectly natural. Good managers will recognise these reactions and should be ready to help and support staff through this negative stage and make steps to help them to accept it eg:

In the 1980's Kent County Council centralised its small typing centres to one large WP centre. The change meant new location; new equipment; new skills. Many staff, particularly the older established staff, were very worried. Some staff also had to drop their shorthand skills and resistance to the change was enormous.

To help some of the staff, the supervisor did 1:1 training on the wordprocessor in the evenings to familiarise them with the equipment. It was also recognised that not all staff would learn at the same rate.

On the other hand, many people may react positively to hearing about changes. They might have reached the stage in their job where they are bored, in a rut or looking for a change.

Their reactions would therefore be:

- Excitement – new challenges, new skills

- Possibility of promotion or growth

- New horizons

- New opportunities – more responsibility

SUMMARY

- As everyone is different so will be their reactions to change

- If change affects us it is personal to us and will depend on other factors present in our lives – eg relocation for someone with no commitments could see this as exciting – whereas it could be a stressful time for someone with family commitments.

DEALING WITH CHANGE

Firstly, accept it is normal to have negative feelings in the first stages of change.

You need time to grieve for what you are losing – colleagues; skills; the familiar things you liked doing; and to ask yourself how you will cope in the future.

Whilst you need time to adjust you cannot stagnate with these feelings. It is not good for you personally, nor for the team or the organisation.

You must start to take the positive steps to reach acceptance of the new environment.

PROFESSIONALLY

- look for areas for your own development

- learn as many new skills as possible – be prepared to drop old skills and take on new ones

- try for promotion

- ask for training

- plan a route for where you want to be

- join a network of people doing similar jobs.

PERSONALLY

- List your strengths and weaknesses.

- Make most of your strengths – build on them.

- Would training improve the weak areas?

- Research all the opportunities now open to you.

- Would you have to give anything up to make the most of these new opportunities?

- Talk through your feelings and aspirations with close colleagues, your manager or Personnel Department. You may have overlooked the obvious. Never be afraid to seek help.

- Don't forget the value of talking to friends and family who see sides of you you don't see yourself.

SUMMARY

- Weigh up the pros and cons of the changes and their effect on you.

- Develop a positive attitude – positive people move forward, negative people stand still.

- If you cannot accept the situation it could be the new environment is not for you. Perhaps this is the time to look for pastures new.

INFLUENCING CHANGE

- Many organisations thinking of making changes realise the benefits of good staff communication. Consulting staff will help to gain their commitment to the change.

- Even though the changes are outside your control you can still have a considerable influence on the way changes are made.

- Be ready to put forward your own ideas. Perhaps you have experienced a situation change in a previous job. Your information could be invaluable.

- Be aware of how others in your team may be feeling. Your own positive attitude will help, whilst adopting a negative attitude drags others down.

- Offer to undertake any research for the changes affecting your department or team.

- Do you have the confidence to offer your own services to train other colleagues on the job?

- Do you have skills in which you are proficient, that you could pass on to others?

- Offer to take on more responsibility during the change. Put forward your own recommendations and feed back to managers how things are going.

The other side of influencing change is where you personally have spotted that a change in the office could benefit everyone.

This could be as a result of experience in a previous job — it worked there so it could work here; or perhaps a new system learned on a training course.

Remember we said earlier that even the smallest change will affect someone and although you are confident it would work they could resist or ignore it. Eg. if you move the external post tray to another position without consulting others, don't be surprised if you find some post in the previous place that missed the deadline. Many things we do at work are a comfortable habit.

How then can you get a change implemented?

- You will need to develop a case to present to your direct manager or your team.

The basis of the presentation should be:

BACKGROUND

- What are we doing now and why do we do it?
- Who is involved?

PROBLEMS

- What are the current problems, drawbacks or difficulties with the system?

PROPOSED CHANGES

- Provide evidence to support change
- Present facts not personal preferences
- List the benefits
- Put forward a proposed plan – how to change from A to B
- Clarify the timings

Remember – whilst presenting your case, be assertive not aggressive. Listen to other people's ideas and suggestions. Be prepared to defend your case but do not become defensive. Be prepared to negotiate and reach a compromise.

SUMMARY

- Change is normal and helps people to progress.
- Ask questions if you are unclear.
- Put forward suggestions.
- Be positive.

DECISION MAKING AND PROBLEM SOLVING

Decision taking and problem solving are for most of us part of our daily work. Some decisions and problems are simple and some are quite complicated. You can, however, learn skills which will help you to solve problems and make the best decisions.

At work, when making decisions, you will usually be faced with a conflict between what is best for the individual, the department and the organisation. Often, the needs of these three areas will conflict and your job will be to balance the conflict so that you make the best decision.

When you are making decisions that only affect you the process is fairly straightforward. It is making decisions which have an impact on others that causes the problems.

WHAT STOPS US MAKING DECISIONS?

- worrying about what others think
- letting others decide
- fear of failure
- thinking there is a perfect solution
- trying to please everyone
- not recognising there is a problem

There are 4 stages you need to go through in order to ensure you are problem solving effectively.

IDENTIFY AND ANALYSE THE PROBLEM

LOOK AT THE OPTIONS

IMPLEMENT YOUR DECISION

EVALUATE THE EFFECTIVENESS OF YOUR DECISION

IDENTIFYING AND ANALYSING THE PROBLEM

The first thing you need to do is recognise that there is a problem in the first place. One definition of a problem is 'the gap between what we have now and what is desirable'.

Often you won't always want to accept that there is a problem because

- it may reflect badly on you

- it might go away if you ignore it

- it isn't your fault that there is a problem

- someone else should sort it out

- you don't know what to do.

However, it is important that you do face problems and make some attempt to sort them out, regardless of your level within the organisation.

First of all you need to ask yourself, is it a crisis or a problem? You won't know this until you have analysed when it needs to be sorted out by.

It helps to analyse the problem if you write it down and answer the following:

- what is the problem?

- when does it need to be sorted out?

- who is involved?

- what are the consequences if you do not deal with it?

- what are the consequences if you do deal with it?

- who can help?

- what is the desired result?

- why did it happen?

Answering these questions will help you to clear your mind and think logically about what to do.

SEPARATING THE PROBLEM FROM THE SYMPTOM

One of the first mistakes that people make is to think that the problem is what they see. In other words, if someone has a headache and simply takes aspirin then they are treating the symptom, ie the headache.

However, it may be that the person has an allergy to chocolate which is causing the headaches. This then is the actual problem, not the headaches, but the allergy to chocolate. If the individual never attempts to find out the problem, ie, the cause of the headaches, then they will not cure the headaches and will simply have to keep taking aspirin.

The same is true at work. The problem may appear to be that telephone messages are not taken down properly. However, that may be only the symptom. The problem may actually be that no one has shown that particular individual how to take down telephone messages properly.

Also, one problem may uncover another problem. For example, you may think that word processing system has crashed. You then discover that the files have not been archived for four months and hundreds of documents have been lost. The problem was not only the system crashing, but also that the archiving had not been done. Sometimes you will discover that the problem that has been uncovered is even bigger than the first one.

PARETO PRINCIPLE

Vilfredo Pareto in the last century did a survey on a number of different civilisations and found invariably 80% of wealth was owned or controlled by 20% of the population.

This rough 80/20 split is very common. Many organisations find that 80% of their business comes from 20% of their customers.

20% of the population drink 80% of the beer that is consumed!

It is often worth seeing if a Pareto split applies to the causes of a problem to save you time in solving the problem. For example, if the word processing system crashes you will need to estimate how many documents you have lost and which of those you will need. It will be fairly safe to concentrate on 20% of the documents/files that you are more likely to need in the short term.

CHALLENGING ASSUMPTIONS

Each time you define a problem, you will tend to build in assumptions that unnecessarily constrain it.

For example, the problem may be 'How to speed up queues in banks'!

The format of this problem assumes:

- that queues in banks are here to stay and that the problem is merely to speed them up

- that people need to visit their bank in person rather than banks providing alternative services.

The technique of challenging assumptions helps us to question problem definitions in order to highlight them and check if they are really necessary constraints.

HOW IT WORKS

Write down the initial definition of the problem (making sure that it's the problem and not the symptom) and underline all the words in it that are debatable. Then take each debatable word in turn and question it.

For example:

- do you merely want to speed up queues?
- is it just queues at the counter that need speeding up?
- should there be queues at all?
- do customers need to visit their bank for all types of services?

After challenging the assumption in the initial definition of the problem you chose to tackle you might then decide that the problem is:

'How to abolish waiting in banks'.

This then is the real problem you need to tackle.

OPTIONS

Having identified and analysed that there is a problem you now need to look at what options and choices you have in order to solve the problem.

In order to identify what options you have:

- ask people – either more senior to you or your colleagues
- ask the customer (if it is a customer problem) if they have any suggestions as to how they would like the problem solved.
- ask anyone who may have encountered a similar problem before how they dealt with it.

Once you have identified a list of possible options you then need to weigh them up. You need to know what the possible consequences are of each option, the pros and cons and what will happen if the decision is the wrong one.

WHAT DO I REALLY WANT?

Sometimes you may be aware of an unsatisfactory situation in a vague sort of way. However, if you come up with a solution you first need to clarify the problem.

A simple technique for doing this is the 'What do I really want?' technique.

HOW IT WORKS

First describe the situation in general terms. Then keep answering the questions 'What do I really want?' and 'What stops me getting it?' until the exact problem has been formulated.

EXAMPLE

Initial description of problem situation:

The merchant's daughter needs to pick a white pebble out of the bag, while she knows there are only 2 black pebbles in the bag.

What do I want ⟶ *What stops me getting it?*
To pick out a white pebble / There are only black pebbles in the bag

So what do I really want? ⟶ *What stops me getting it?*
To introduce a white pebble / The money lender would into the bag / spot me doing this.

So what do I really want? ⟶ *What stops me getting it?*
To make it appear a white / Cannot introduce a white
pebble was picked out of / pebble into the bag.
the bag

So what do I really want?
To leave one black pebble in
the bag.

So, the first stage in identifying options often means actually trying to establish exactly what it is you want to achieve.

Once you have decided what it is you want to achieve and you have identified a list of possible solutions think of the implications of choosing any one particular option.

Write down the pros and cons in 2 columns. If there are two main alternatives, which there often are, make two columns which allow you to write the pros and cons in each.

EXAMPLE

The problem is that a long standing, very valued customer has rung to complain that a software package that she has bought from your organisation is not quite what she expected. She is quite annoyed. You know that it states quite clearly in the product brochure exactly what the software package is and what it is capable of doing. Your organisation has a policy that states that in normal circumstances customers will not be given a refund for purchases of software packages unless the package is proven to be faulty.

It is lunch time and your immediate manager is out of the office attending a management training course with all of the other managers in the organisation and will not be returning until tomorrow

---

customer has said that unless you agree to a full refund, she will cancel all future orders. She wants confirmation of a full refund in writing today.

You have consulted with your immediate team and it is quite clear that you cannot risk calling the customer's bluff because they do spend a lot of money with your organisations. You have therefore identified 3 possible solutions to the problem.

1 Agree to a full refund

2 Agree to a partial refund

3 Ask her to return the software package to you and you will exchange it for one that more nearly meets her needs.

OPTION 1 – AGREE TO A FULL REFUND

PROS	CONS
Will satisfy the customer	Will cost your company £2500
You are less likely to lose their business	Goes against the company policy
	Danger of setting a precedent
	Your manager might not like this decision.

OPTION 2 – AGREE TO A PARTIAL REFUND

PROS	CONS
May keep the customer quiet	Will cost the company £1500
A compromise solution	May set a precedent
	Goes against company policy

OPTION 3 – REPLACE SOFTWARE PACKAGE WITH ONE MORE SUITABLE

PROS   CONS

May satisfy the customer
Will keep the business
Will not cost the organisation
money

You can see quite clearly from listing the pros and cons what appears to be the most suitable decision to take.

It is always better to actually write down the pros and cons. This does not necessarily take much time. Sometimes it can take just a few minutes. So it is always worth spending the time to actually write it down.

There may, however, be times when you do not have much time for detailed analysis of the options and you must have the confidence to take a risk and make a decision.

Making your choice can be difficult, so find the right balance between spending time evaluating the options and not allowing the problem to get out of hand. Learn to trust your judgement.

Always be sure to note down somewhere what you decided and why. That way if anyone challenges your decision at a later date, you will easily be able to answer their queries and justify your decision.

IMPLEMENTATION

Once you have made your decision – DO IT.

What you will need at this stage is confidence and tact. Confidence you will gain by having thoroughly thought the problem through and practice. Tact is gained by thinking about how the other person feels.

Even if you are not totally sure, remember that everybody takes risks, and only risk takers actually progress.

Decisions do take courage. Be committed and stick to the decision you have made.

EVALUATION

Evaluation is important in order to see that the problem has actually been solved as well as for your own learning process.

If the problem was not solved, find out why not and then re-think the situation.

If it was solved, what consequences were there?

DEALING WITH OTHER PEOPLE'S PROBLEMS

Do not allow other people to off load their problems on to you unless it is something that only you can deal with. This is because if you are constantly solving other people's problems for them they will never learn how to solve them for themselves.

It is often very tempting to tell someone more junior or less experienced than us what we would do.

Avoid saying 'leave the problem with me', but at the same time do not ignore the fact that they have highlighted a problem to you.

To encourage them to identify and solve their own problems:

- ask open questions such as 'what options do you have?'

- use 'WE' language if appropriate. eg, 'What can WE do to solve this?' or if you are trying to give them ownership ' what can YOU do about it?'

- get them to think it through eg, 'how is Fred likely to react to this?'
- gain their agreement to what the problem actually is
- perhaps get them to talk to someone else other than you

What should you say if they have suggested a solution that you know won't work?

- Don't tell them that they are wrong.
- Ask 'What else could you do?'
- Encourage them to think it through eg: 'What would happen if you took that particular course of action?'

In other words, discuss possible solutions, act as a sounding board, point them in the right direction, but don't make their problems your own.

NEGOTIATION

Sometimes when you are confronted with a problem the best solution is for you to negotiate with the individual/s concerned.

All of us negotiate, whether it is at home or at work.

Negotiation is basically attempting to find a solution that everybody is happy with, but not necessarily a solution that everyone finds perfect. Negotiation should result in a solution to a problem that causes the least upset to everyone and is the most acceptable to all concerned. Remember that you are looking for the **least worst option**.

STAGES OF NEGOTIATION

1 DEFINE YOUR OBJECTIVES
What is it that you want?
What do you hope for at best?
What would you settle for?

Eg, you want to take 5 weeks holiday to travel to Australia during a very busy period during the year. You hope that you will be given permission to take the full 5 weeks, however, you are prepared to settle for 4.

2 PREPARATION

- Assess the situation (what are people's reactions likely to be?)

- When would be the best time to discuss, eg, immediately, or can it wait until you have thought things through more?

- Book a room if appropriate.

- Discuss with others who may be directly involved, and those indirectly involved (eg your boss)

- Have any documents ready that you might need.

- Think of facts that you might need to bear in mind first.

2 COMMUNICATE – CHOOSE WHICH STYLE OF NEGOTIATION
There are 5 different negotiation styles.

Compromise
Accommodate
Withdraw
Collaborate
Defeat

COMPROMISE

This is where you are aiming for a win/win situation where both parties get at least a part of what they want. That means both people being prepared to give up something in order that both gain.

ACCOMMODATE

This is where you take into account the other person's needs and agree to change something or do something differently in order to accommodate the other person.

WITHDRAW

This is where it is clear to you that you are not gaining anything from your discussion and you are can see that there is no chance of getting what you want so you decide to simply back down.

COLLABORATE

This is where you work together with someone to come up with a joint solution. It is different from compromise in that you may not necessarily have to 'give' up anything. In collaborating you work together on the problem so that any solutions are jointly arrived at and agreed.

DEFEAT

This is generally used in a crisis situation where you do not have time to go into lengthy discussions or explanations, you simply have to make a decision which overrules the needs of the other person.

SUMMARY

Even if you do not have a great deal of experience you can ensure that you are successful in problem solving and decision taking if you are methodical in your approach.

DO

- Concentrate

- Think logically and go through the stages of decision taking

- Be honest (was it your fault?)

- Be positive

- Be open to criticism

- Accept problems

- Be patient

- Recognise your limits – you may need to pass the problem over to someone else

- Be open minded, particularly to other people's solutions

- Be willing to learn from the problem

- Have the courage to try or start again

- Keep the problem in perspective

- Have a sense of humour when it's been solved

- Talk to other people about the problem

- Be confident

- Get off to a good start in your communication by

explaining why there is a problem and why you have decided to take that action that you have.

DON'T

- Be over-sensitive
- Take it personally
- Be over emotional
- Be tunnel-visioned, there is always a way out
- Be negative
- Blame others
- Panic
- Hide or cover up either the problem or your actions
- Put off decisions or procrastinate.

BALANCING HOME AND WORK

Ten years ago you probably wouldn't have found a chapter on balancing home and work in a book on administration skills. It just goes to show how things have changed.

Much of this change is due to the increasing number of women in the workplace. In general, it is women who have felt most keenly the need to juggle the demands of traditional roles in the home with the demands of work.

Of course not all administrators are women and of course it isn't just women who are concerned about balance in their lives. The good news is that increasingly both men and women recognise the importance of a healthy sense of proportion.

WALKING THE TIGHTROPE

We have already talked about 'balancing' and 'juggling'. Both imply some sort of dexterity along with the possibility of either falling over or dropping the lot.

Most of you know when you have got it wrong.

EITHER:

You spend most of your time at work, or thinking about it. Your private life is non-existent. You barely recognise your home, or anyone else who might occupy it.

OR:

Demands in your private life require your presence, your energy and your undivided attention – whether they are children, partners, parents, or some other consuming interest.

Either way, the bottom line is CONFLICT and GUILT. You end up with clashing priorities and a queue of resentful people to sort out.

STRUGGLING WITH JUGGLING

Feeling torn is the first sign that things are not right. Clearly, you must allow for temporary imbalances: the rush of work around budget time, organising a major conference, winning a key client, working on a special project or dealing with an office move. On the home front, it could be coping with *life* events: marriage, children, sickness, bereavement, job loss, house moves. These things come along periodically and for most of us the energy focus is temporary.

The trouble starts when this lop-sided state of affairs becomes a permanent feature. When, for example, you find yourself working in an organisation where people are expected, as a matter of course, to arrive early and stay late; to take work home and work weekends. Conversely the demands could be stacked on the home front when you are faced with the long-term commitment of elderly parents, young children or a similarly demanding domestic life.

The choices are the same for both men and women but the conflicts remain the most acute for women. Women are still perceived (or they perceive themselves) as the primary carers and homemakers. This is changing – but slowly.

Here are some examples of the sort of mess you can get ourself into:

EXAMPLE:

Kevin, a clerk in the Civil Service, took on a two year posting. It was a good career step but it meant moving to London. He has three children under six and is keen to be part of their growing up. He and his wife decided that they would all move rather than endure weekend commuting which was the alternative.

Kevin finds that with a young family he is severely disadvantaged in the new post. Long hours are the norm; after-work socialising is an important part of staying 'in-the-know'. He feels caught in the middle, pleasing no-one with pressure on both sides to Be There.

EXAMPLE:

Alice, on the other hand, has no children but she does have a partner to care for and home to maintain. Both she and her partner commute long distances to work. They leave the house well before 7am and are seldom home before 8pm. After a full days work in a demanding job as an accounts clerk, Alice has to plan and cook an evening meal. Her weekends are spent catching up, washing, ironing, cleaning, watching her partner play football and fitting in duty visits to respective parents. On top of this they are active members of the Residents Association and Alice acts as Secretary to the football club.

Alice finds that far from being refreshed after the weekend she is exhausted. Both her work and her relationship are beginning to suffer.

EXAMPLE:

Marion, a single parent with two young children, works as a secretary in a large legal practice. She enjoys her job. Long hours are an accepted part of legal work but there is the incentive of earning overtime. Organising and paying for child care to cope with her irregular hours is a major difficulty. During the week she sees little of her children. Weekends are spent catching up on routine housework.

Marion feels guilty about seeing so little of her children. This is made worse because she has little time or energy for socialising and feels increasingly isolated in her private life.

So, what can Kevin, Alice, Marion, you and I and the thousands like us do to avoid this damaging conflict?

GET ACROBATIC

For a start forget about *avoiding* and start thinking about *managing* the conflict – and come to terms with the fact that managing it is a *constant* process and not a one off re-distribution of weight. Look for the ability in yourself to make healthy choices and retain a sense of proportion. This will be different for different people. Knowing what is right FOR YOU is the key.

It comes down to:

- being clear about what is important to you

- being able to communicate this to others

- being able to negotiate with others to protect what is important to you

When you read the chapters in this book on stress and time management, on decision making and assertiveness you will recognise these fundamental principles coming through time and time again.

STEP 1 – WORKING OUT WHAT IS IMPORTANT

Knowing what is important in your life is one of the first steps in gaining control. Here are some areas of life which people have identified as being important to them:

- job/career success

- financial security

- children

- friends

- partner

- other relatives

- hobbies/interests
- health
- politics
- religion/spiritual self
- education
- self development
- voluntary/community work
- home

Now choose SIX of these areas which are important to you RIGHT NOW and list them in order of priority.

Taking the time to think about what you value – your priorities in life – and then seeing how much time you are presently devoting to these is a thought-provoking exercise. The next step is to go beyond thought to **action**.

STEP 2 – SLICING THE CAKE

One of the most helpful things you can do for yourself is to take an honest look at how you divide up your time at the moment. How are you slicing your own cake? Try this simple exercise. It is important not to think too hard or to try and be too precise. The exercise is designed to be impressionistic:

Take a piece of paper and draw a circle. Now, in very general terms, divide it up into four parts:

WORK – paid or unpaid

CHORES – general maintenance tasks

LEISURE – things you do with others for pleasure or to please

> ME – things you do entirely for yourself (they may
> or may not involve others)

The way you slice up the cake should represent just how it
feels for you right now, overall. Don't try to limit it to any
particular time span. Forget sleeping, for the purpose of
this exercise it is built in! The circle below belongs to a
married female office manager – hers is a typical example
of a working woman in the '90s.

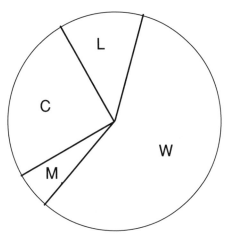

M – Me, W – Work, L – Leisure, C – Chores.

Having looked at how you are spending your time,
decide whether you are comfortable with what you see. If
so, congratulations – skip the rest of the chapter. If not,
put dotted lines in where you would like the slices to be.

Just this simple exercise illustrates graphically an
important and obvious point: time is *finite*. You cannot, as
one person on a workshop put it, 'make the circle bigger'.
Giving yourself more time in one section means taking a
bit out of another – something has to give – or more likely,
you have to give up something.

STEP 3 – ADJUSTING THE SEGMENTS

Most people get the balance by cutting down on the Work and Chores slices to make larger bits of Leisure and Me-time. Examining the segments for some 'slack' is a good place to start.

CHORES

Although things are changing for the better, it is probably true to say that this section will still have more interest and relevance to women. What can you do to spend less time and energy on the drudge in your life?

Try this test. It is called '*I have to, or else. . .*'. You need to be ruthlessly honest with yourself.

Make a list of all the things you *have* to do at home. When you have done this, go through the list and really challenge yourself – or even better, find someone else to challenge you. Ask, WHY you have to do each of the things. Also, most importantly, ask WHY it has to be YOU who does them? In other words, will everything come to a complete standstill if either you fail to do the thing at all, or someone else does it?

Having gone through this exercise, you might accept that you are doing a great many things because you choose to and/or that you are just clinging on to some ancient deeply embedded belief that you SHOULD.

You do need to reckon with the power of past conditioning. These are the kind of things people on workshops come up with under the chores section:

> '*I have to keep a tidy house because it worries me if it isn't*'

> '*I have to iron everything because it makes the fabric feel nice*'

'I have to do the cooking because no one else will'

'I have to entertain because other people entertain me/us'

'I have to do the home improvements because I/we can't afford to get anyone else in'

'I have to see my family every weekend because they would be disappointed if I didn't'

The list is endless. Notice the flimsiness of some of the excuses. In themselves, none of the above are necessarily causes for concern or conflict. By all means iron everything (including, as one person told us, the laces on the children's trainers) but the minute you feel resentful, torn, angry or guilty it is time to stop and examine just what you are doing with your time.

Here are some things to consider:

- *Own attitudes:*
  Examine your own attitudes. For those of you hooked into regular cleaning, raising your dirt tolerance is a first step to getting the balance. Remember Shirley Conran's Law of Housework, i.e. it expands to fill the available time. Lowering your culinary standards might be another strategy for those of you who feel compelled to spend hours slaving over the stove (unless of course you find this activity relaxing and balancing in itself). This does not mean having to eat badly.

- *Assertiveness Training*
  Assertiveness is a wonderful tool for re-negotiating boundaries. It helps you clarify what you can and cannot do. See the section below on using other people for examples of where assertive conversations might be needed in the home.

● *Using other people – Support networks*
We all need other people. Having a wide range of contacts is useful emotionally as well as practically. Here we are concerned with the practical. You can use other people to help you cut down on the 'chore' section in all sorts of ways. Two obvious ones:

a) Employing extra help
Paying someone else to do some of your chores is an obvious solution to over commitment. It is not an option that is open to all of us but it is open to more of us than you would think.

Think about it. Paying someone else means that you make the clear choice to sacrifice some of your earnings to win more time to pursue other activities.

(The danger is, of course, that you spend even *more* time at work earning more to pay for more people and gadgets to sustain a labour-saving, time-saving lifestyle that enables you to cope with increasing work pressure . . . a paradoxical and perilous spiral).

b) *Enlisting 'voluntary' help – delegating*
Those of us 'sharing living quarters' need to make quite sure that the ground rules are clear and that everyone is pulling their weight equally. You often hear people being encouraged to delegate in the context of home as well as work.

We have already said it is worth questioning why you are the only person carrying out certain 'life maintenance functions'. Sharing the load is one thing, but ideally you want share accountability as well. It may be great to have someone help with the shopping and hoovering but it is probably still you who makes the decisions, writes the lists and sets the quality standards.

Delegation means you retain accountability. Why not take things a stage further and re-write the job description. This means others take on the whole thing without referral to you. The advantage of this is that it is one less thing to worry about. The downside is that standards may not be entirely to your liking. You can't have everything – the moral of the chapter.

LEISURE AND ME-TIME

Balance is about variety – a bit of everything. Fitting it all in is the problem.

- *Scheduling time for pleasure*
  Anyone who has been on a time management course will know that blocking out time to do certain things increases the likelihood of getting them done.

  Increasingly, people are seeing the effectiveness of using their work diary in more realistic way and are including home events and life goals. In other words, scheduling in advance, time to spend on the activities and people that are important to you and not allowing the blank spaces to be gobbled up on demand. '*I haven't had time. . .to take a holiday*' is a common complaint. Put it in. Only you can make it happen.

WORK

Clearly all the above principles apply equally to the workplace. Time management is a boom business; there are countless books and courses to help you do it better. Simple exercises like '*I have to or else. . .*' are good for identifying where you might be losing time and energy unnecessarily.

Harder to cope with is an organisational culture that expects, accepts and subtly rewards working long and unsociable hours. This is the macho world of all-night sittings, clinching the deal in the early hours, not seeing friends and family for days.

Most of us are prepared to accept the bottom line; the reality that there will be peaks in our working lives when we will have to pull out all the stops. The difficulty comes when these working practices are glamorised as part of a *real* job and getting-on means conforming to them. If you are working in this sort of environment it is doubly hard to admit to, let alone begin to accommodate, the needs of your private life.

There are ways round this dilemma, some more ingenious than other. Take for example, the apocryphal story of the City organisation where you need two jackets – one to leave hanging on your chair to indicate presence, the other to wear to go home in. Perhaps women should consider having two handbags. . .'Her bag's here, she must be around. . .'.

On a more serious note, it would be better if you did not have to resort to such ruses in the first place. Although it is hard to cope with, it is important that you address the problem for yourself. There are things you can do and choices you can make:

- *Question*

  People tend to subscribe blindly instead of questioning:

  - What do you actually **produce** during these extra hours?

  - Are there more flexible ways in which you could work and still be equally productive.

- *Set an Example*
  Use the hours at work to **produce** and encourage others to do the same – especially if you supervise anyone, formally or informally. Break the pattern of staying late regularly.

- *Respect Private Time – Your Own and Other People's*
  Wherever possible use normal working hours for telephone calls, meetings, seminars and courses. However tempting, avoid setting up anything before breakfast, after work or at weekends.

- *Discuss with your Manager*
  Here is where you can use your assertiveness to have useful conversations. You need to be able to make it clear that whilst you are willing, co-operative and committed to the success of the organisation you also have other interests and commitments that require your attention.

EXAMPLE:

Anna came into a new job where it was accepted that everyone put in 100%, worked all hours and travelled extensively, often in their own time and at weekends. Anna made a stand about travelling on Sundays. The initial reaction was incredulous and hostile from both management and colleagues – 'How do you suppose we'd stay in business if we all thought like you'. Anna persisted, pointing out that by thinking ahead, being clear with clients and rescheduling jobs they could virtually eliminate Sunday travel and still deliver the service. It worked. Sunday travel is no longer accepted as the norm.

- *Discuss with your Colleagues*
  Bringing balance into the work place concerns
  everyone. How family friendly is your
  organisation? Does it have policies that allow
  people to attend to all aspects of their lives without
  limiting their career prospects?

- *Challenge*
  Start asking why and suggesting why not? This
  takes courage and − as with anything different −
  one person to start. Watch sheep being herded
  through a narrow gap − it just takes one free spirit
  to set the others thinking along the same lines.

SUMMARY

The good news is that it looks as if the days of the
'corporation person' are numbered − if not done. Making a
LIFE as well as a living has become a general concern and
an increasingly acceptable demand. This climate should
make it easier for us all to take a long hard look at what we
are doing and begin to take action to check any
imbalances. A permanently lop-sided life leads to
malfunctioning in one area or another. We need to accept
that balancing implies *continuous* corrective action.
    To recap:

- Work out what is important to you

- Work out how you want to slice up your cake

- Set some limits at home and at work

- Take corrective action at the first signs of wobble

- Combine the tips in this Chapter with the stress
  plan in Chapter 8. The only way to do it, is to do
  it.

UNDERSTANDING BASIC BUDGETING

THE IMPORTANCE OF FINANCIAL CONTROLS

All organisations, both public and private, need to operate successfully financially in order to do all the things they want to. Even non-profit making organisations, such as charities, local authorities etc, need to achieve a surplus or profit in order to survive.

It is not enough for an organisation to break even. Profits are important because:

- No matter how good an organisation is at budgeting and achieving budgets, it is almost impossible for them to guarantee that they will exactly achieve a break-even position, ie, to have their income exactly cover their expenditure.

- If an organisation was only aiming to break even and consistently made a loss (ie, expenditure is higher than income) then eventually it will have to close down.

- If an organisation wants to expand, to do new things, employ more staff, give pay rises, buy new machinery and equipment it needs to have funds to do that. The best way for an organisation to get these funds is to provide them themselves, out of their profit or surplus.

- If an organisation has shareholders, these shareholders will expect to be paid dividends. Dividends cannot be paid unless the organisation is making a profit.

- Most organisations have to pay corporation tax to the government which helps to pay for Education, Health, Defence and so on.

PROFIT AND LOSS ACCOUNTS

A profit and loss account deals with measuring the viability of a business. In other words, is it doing well enough to stay in business or in the case of the public sector, to justify its existence?

CASH FLOW

Even though an organisation may be in profit on paper, it is essential that it has enough money in the bank to pay its bills. For example, it may be owed a substantial sum by its customers, but if they haven't paid and the money isn't in the bank the organisation may not be able to pay its salaries, bills and its suppliers.

Because organisations spread the capital cost of fixed assets such as equipment over their expected 'life' (so that one year's profits is not adversely impacted versus another relative to the use of the asset), this is another reason why cash flow and profit are not the same.

When looking at the profit and loss account we also need to take into account the cash position of the organisation. In other words, if the profit is good, but the money isn't in the bank, the organisation knows that it needs to take action.

THE BALANCE SHEET

The Balance Sheet is basically a record of the assets that an organisation owns and the wealth of the business. It also records the sources of funding that the organisation has, for example, the amount of money contributed by shareholders (known as Capital), retained profit or reserves (the money that the organisation has kept to one side and not paid to shareholders) and any long term loans that it has.

BUDGETS

A budget enables an organisation to measure its performance against the financial plan that it has for its future. Normally the yearly budget will be linked to the longer term financial plan which will be tied into the aims of the organisation.

A budget means that the organisation can decide in advance what it wants to spend its money on and how much money it needs to make in order to buy new equipment etc and to make a profit.

During the year, the organisation will have to report how well it is achieving against its budget. Many organisations will forecast in advance how well they think they are likely to do compared to what the budget says they must do. This process becomes more important as the organisation comes to the end of its financial year when the budget may no longer be an up to date guide to predicting financial results.

THE DEPARTMENT BUDGETING CONTEXT

When creating a departmental budget, you have to be clear that what you are putting down is not just a 'wish list'. All departmental budgets have to be tied in to the overall needs of the organisation. It is not uncommon to find that a department that makes a lot of money is not allowed to buy new equipment because the money is needed to fund another part of the organisation. All budgets need to take into account the overheads of the organisation (that is the cost of salaries, electricity, telephone, maintenance of the buildings etc).

Normally allocations of money will be decided only when all of the departmental draft budgets have been added together. Only then can the organisation see how much money there is on the Profit and Loss Account and the Balance Sheet.

At the beginning of the budgeting process, the organisation will usually have a rough idea of how much money it needs to make and where it hopes to find the money from. It will also have some idea of what investment it wants to make, ie, new machinery, more staff. The person doing the budget will need this information in order to put the departmental budget together. They will also need to take into account things like inflation, expected price rises, pay increases and so on.

ZERO BASED BUDGETING

A zero based budget is when a department is asked to start with the assumption that it has no money to spend unless it can be justified from scratch. In other words, as if they had to start the department all over again.

This helps departments to rethink the way that they have done things in the past and come up with new and better approaches to achieving their business objectives.

THE SEVEN STEPS OF THE BUDGET PROCESS

Having a budget gives the department a plan to follow. Even if circumstances change, it is considerably easier to make adjustments to a basic plan which is sound, rather than to have to start afresh because the budget wasn't properly done in the first place and now bears little relation to reality.

The seven steps to a successful budget are:

1   Defining objectives
2   Defining responsibility
3   Gathering information
4   Deciding what to submit
5   Testing and checking
6   Gaining approval
7   Living with the budget

1 DEFINING OBJECTIVES

The budget objectives need to link in to the longer term plans of the business as a whole and dovetail with the budgets of other departments. The department needs to be absolutely clear about what it wants to achieve in the year and what changes there are likely to be during the budget year.

2 DEFINING RESPONSIBILITIES

The department needs to know what its resources are. The list should cover:

- People, including those directly within the department as well as any temporary or sub-contracted staff

- Systems of work and data processing methods (changes here can have considerable impact on a department's expenditure line)

- Material supplies

- Energy costs (eg, electricity)

- Outside services (eg, printing)

- Information about the use of space and charges (eg rent or mortgage).

The last three items are sometimes budgeted centrally and are allocated to the department rather than budgeted by them.

3 GATHERING INFORMATION

The department will also need to have the following information before preparing the budget:

- How did it perform against this year's budget?

- Does this year's actual expenditure give enough guidance as to what the department is likely to spend money on next year?

- What is the organisation's policy on how to budget? Some organisations have rigid budgets which they demand to be met. Others see the budget as simply a set of guidelines which may be altered during the year, provided this can be sensibly justified.

The budget is normally drawn up 3 to 4 months before the start of the next financial year. However, to make next year's budget realistic, you will need to calculate what you expect to actually achieve against budget for this financial year in detail. This will help you to make your predictions for the next financial year more accurate.

It is important, therefore, to make sure that you have an up to date picture of how well you have done financially against your budget for this year. This will mean that you will need to keep your manager informed of your income and expenditure on a regular basis, not simply the amounts, but what for and why. You will also need to have an idea of how much you expect to earn/spend next year based on what has happened this year.

4 DECIDING WHAT TO SUBMIT

The first task is to calculate roughly what you will earn and spend by the end of the next financial year, based on what you have actually done this year.

This is the basis for working out the detail of the budget. Having taken into account the organisational needs and aims, you may well find that your own spending patterns vary slightly. For example, you may know that although this year you have spent a certain sum on running a company car for a salesperson, next year that salesperson will be doing fewer miles, so you may make an adjustment to that part of the budget.

You may also anticipate that whereas last year you got 20% of your income from selling X product, this year it is likely to come from Y product. Or, that last year you earned 80% of your income in the first 8 months of the year, but next year, because of a change in your customers, you expect to earn only 60% in the first 8 months.

All of this information affects your monthly budget and

it is important to keep a note of these reasons while you are budgeting in case you need to explain or justify your budget later. It is also useful to look back on when you are comparing actual to budget next year. You can then see where you may have misjudged.

Some of the budget will not be based on precise information. Sometimes you will have to take a 'best guess'. Do avoid making your guess a complete 'stab in the dark' by consulting with your colleagues before allocating an exact sum to the income or expenditure line.

5 TESTING AND CHECKING

Once you have identified your basic budget, you then need to see if it makes sense. Does it compare favourably to previous years' budgets? Is it realistic and achievable? Are you spending the right money on the right things? Do each of the different items of income and expenditure match each other? For example, have you budgeted an income of £50,000 on X product but have an expenditure line of £55,000 which is the cost of marketing and selling it.

Once you feel that your budget is overall about right, you then need to break down into greater detail what it looks like on a month by month basis. At this stage you may discover that by breaking it down month by month, your year end total is unrealistic or not generous enough.

You can rarely simply take your overall year figure and divide it by 12. Usually you will find that there are seasonal variations.

Sometimes you will know that you have a certain expenditure to pay out, but you cannot say in advance which month the money will be paid out of. In that case, the best thing to do is to spread it out over several months so that no month looks totally unrepresentative.

It is also important to know the process by which expenditure will be reported in the monthly budget varience statements issued by the finance function. Some organisations only report expenditure as have taken place when the cheque is paid out (linking the budget to cash flow), others when the invoice is received (linking it to the profit & loss account) or it might be on the basis of when the commitment is made, eg by placing an order so that the uncommitted budget spend is revealed (this can be important for organisations such as those funded on a cash basis by government, as unspent budgets may be lost at year-end). Therefore unless you know how and when the expenditure will be reported, it will be difficult to show the correct timing of expenditure proposed in the budget.

6 WINNING APPROVAL

Once the department budget has been worked out by the manager, it will be submitted to the manager's boss and ultimately to the Finance Department.

- It is important that the budget submitted is more than simply accurate figures. Presentation is important and the budget needs to be submitted in house style with all supporting documentation.

- It is very unusual for the first budget submitted to be accepted. What most often happens is that the department is given back the budget and asked to make amendments to either the income or expenditure lines. It is therefore important that any notes made during the budgeting process are kept in case they are needed for reference.

- If you can show how the budget figures were

built up, then your proposals are more likely to be accepted provided the basis is shown to be sound. it will also be helpful when it comes to monitoring actual expenditure (in step 7) because the impact of any change in circumstances which is likely to lead to changed expenditure can be demonstrated.

- Once the final budget has been submitted, the organisation will add all the departments' budgets together to make sure that they add up to the original whole and that they fit in with the business plan. Sometimes, departments have to accept budget changes that they do not agree with, however, the organisation needs to look at the whole not just the individual departments.

7 LIVING WITH THE BUDGET

- Once the budget is in place it needs to be monitored on a regular basis. This way, any unusual variances can be spotted before they become a major problem.

- It is not enough to look at what has happened. The department's manager will also be expected to calculate how s/he expects the department to do in the next few months compared to the budget.

- You will need to keep your manager informed of any particular variances against budget that you expect as well as keep strict records of what you have spent.

- You will also need to keep a note of any goods, materials etc that you have ordered and that your department will have to pay for, including internal ones. It is very easy to order something, receive an invoice and pass it for payment and miss the fact that you never actually received the goods. Similarly, it is extremely easy to send a customer some goods and forget to invoice for them.

- Keep track of money in and out so that your organisation can maintain control of its cash flow. This means coding up expenditure which identifies where the money is being spent and what it is being spent on. For example, E17 numbers may mean hospitality bills, E45 numbers may mean travel expenditure, E28 numbers may mean the cost of external stationery and so on.

- It is essential that you understand and make a note of what you have spent money on and who or which department is going to pay for it, especially if it is not your own. This will help the manager to keep a detailed track of expenditure and help to identify any errors.

ACTION TO HELP ACHIEVE THE DEPARTMENTAL BUDGET

- Keep records about how the budget works in your organisation.

- Keep notes of any significant changes to the budget throughout the year.

- Begin preparing your own budget information in advance so that when your manager begins the budgeting process you will have the information needed to hand.

- Keep a note of what your reasons were for deciding that you needed to spend or expected to earn a certain amount of money.

- Look at the monthly actual income and expenditure against the budget so that if you spot anything unusual you can point it out to your manager.

- Keep your manager regularly informed of any changes you expect in the budget well in advance of those changes actually occurring.

INFORMATION TECHNOLOGY AND ITS IMPACT ON SUPPORT STAFF

THE HISTORY OF THE OFFICE

The telephone, typewriter and telex have not changed in basic design for over a hundred years. Mechanisation of offices started in the second half of the 19th century. Taking pen to paper was still the main technology of office work. But, by the turn of the century a number of mechanical devices had an established place in the office; Morse's telegraph, Bell's telephone, Edison's dictating machine and the typewriter.

TWENTIETH CENTURY OFFICE DEVELOPMENT

The first 50 years of this century also brought the teletypewriter, automatic telephone switching, ticker tape, the electric typewriter, duplicating machines, photocopiers, adding machines and calculators, tape recorders for dictation, small offset printing presses, data processing equipment operated with punched paper cards.

There was rapid expansion in the volume of office communication and people employed in white collar work.

By the mid-1960s most large businesses had turned to computers to facilitate such routine back office tasks as storing payroll data and issuing cheques, controlling inventory and monitoring the payment of bills. Remote terminals, consisting of either a keyboard or teletypewriter began to appear.

By the late 60s and early 70s there was the advent of

inexpensive copiers, minicomputers, electronic switchboards and word processors, then towards the end of the 70s the microcomputer.

During the 1980s the growth of information technology meant very few offices were without personal computers (PCs) facsimile machines (fax), sophisticated photocopiers, electronic mail, and dedicated telephone systems.

BASICALLY THE OFFICE HAS NOT CHANGED

An anthropologist visiting an office today would see much the same as fifty years ago. He would see people:

- reading

- writing on paper

- handling mail

- talking with one another, – face to face and on the telephone

- typing

- operating calculators

- dictating

- filing and retrieving files from metal cabinets.

However, since the introduction of computers in schools in the 1970s most people see the keyboard as an office tool and not something only secretaries, typists and administrators use.

Nowadays both men and women operate computers, typewriters and word processors. The keyboard is as normal a tool to be found in the office or home as the telephone was thirty years ago. Some keyboards propel self-contained devices for engineers, scientists, business executives. All types of businesses depend on the use of a keyboard attachment for computation, data analysis, scheduling and communications.

In the early days of workstation development most of them were devised to serve a single purpose. Now like people, they multi-task. Instead of the single task of preparing text they can also access the stock market, make air travel reservations. The stockbrokers' terminal started out as a replacement for the ticker tape, the word processor as a replacement for the typewriter.

The evolution of the typewriter took more than 100 years. The evolution of the personal computer has taken less than a decade.

THE THREE AGES OF OFFICE LIFE

- The **pre-industrial** age
- The **industrial** age
- The **information** age.

We are in the **information** age now.

The pre-industrial and industrial ages depends largely on performance of individuals, without much benefit from systematic work organisation or machines. The industrial office organises people to serve the needs of a rigid production system and its machines. The information age office has the potential of combining systems and machines to the benefit of both individual workers and their clients.

HOW IT AFFECTS ADMINISTRATORS

The days of the copy typist, filing clerk, data entry clerk, wages clerk and invoice typist are numbered. Changes are occurring in the following ways:

- Secretaries whose sole function is to be a word processor – (i.e. shorthand to pad, voice to machine, interpreter to keyboard, typewriter or word processor,) days are somewhat limited.

- The three components that formed the role of full time secretary a century ago are fast disappearing. The author keying in their own text, together with electronic filing has eradicated these three parts of the job.

- Administration staff whose sole jobs it is to input information into paper records are now almost extinct. In all aspects of office life the machine takes the place of the dreary task.

- Companies have flatter structures. A whole trench of information managers has disappeared. Whereas just a few years ago if a Managing Director wanted to know the latest figures on imports or exports, or how many graduates had been recruited, s/he would ask an information manager a few floors below. Nowadays s/he or his/her assistant can bring on to the screen up-to-date reliable information at the touch of a few buttons.

- However, a filter is still required if a manager is to make the most productive use of his or her time. Despite much of the routine speeded up or passed to another, there will still be some tasks on which the managers' time and qualifications would be wasted. Certainly the creation or construction of longer documents may well be left to a secretary, as would their distribution.

- New technology allows secretaries and administrative staff to take on more of the managerial workload. The secretary or administrator will become an even more important point of contact between the manager and other parts of the system – which in fact is just what happens in today's non-automated systems. As the hardware and software advances, the secretary or administrator, as in today's offices, will probably be the first to have mastered the idiosyncrasies and constraints of the system better and sooner than the manager.

- As more administrative staff become familiar with the ever newer technology in the office, so their roles will change. As their knowledge increases of the new technology systems, so their jobs will evolve.

- Increased knowledge of graphics packages, spreadsheet packages, setting up of systems, updating databases.

- Drawing up presentations, mixing images and text on screen, taking on the responsibility of running applications programmes for managers and controlling and retrieving information from a database. All of these tasks will change the role of the secretary or administrator.

- Some larger organisations are dispensing with the job of secretary for some of their middle management. A great deal of the normal traditional functions of a secretary or administrator is being superseded by technology.

- With the correct equipment it is very easy for

managers to manage a diary (book appointments for oneself as well as others) communicate within organisations through workstations (electronic mail) key-in memos, letters and reports, painlessly and effortlessly.

Why have a secretary to take the phone calls and answer the odd query in the office?

CHANGES IN THE NEXT TEN YEARS

TELEWORKING – WORKING FROM SOMEWHERE OTHER THAN THE COMMUNAL OFFICE.

For most of us offices can be where we decide to be. Today's manager has the capability to work from anywhere and to increase the office mobility. Portable workstations, hand held lap tops, electronic notebooks, all these make for office information systems to be available quicker, easier, cheaper and faster virtually anywhere.

- Portable workstations bring the lifting of the restriction that there is no longer any need to assemble all the workers at the same place at the same time. The office can be anywhere – at home (teleworking) visiting a client, in an hotel, on a train, even in an aeroplane. Essentially anywhere the worker happens to be.

- Communicating electronically with the central office, this will extend the range of places where written and numerical material can be generated, stored, retrieved, manipulated and communicated.

- Fibre optics have brought about combined text and image conferencing.

- Teleconferencing means valuable time and expense is not spent on travelling to meetings. Or on the costly maintenance of buildings and meeting rooms. This therefore increases the efficiency of those meetings that do take place.

- We are familiar with the use of the telephone, and know that it is no longer necessary to go to someone's office to write or dictate a letter, to read mail or find something in a file. Now the job is no longer tied to the flow of paper across a designated desk; it is tied to the worker alone. The individual can therefore organise his or her own time and decide when and where the work is to be done.

- All these factors leave the administrator or secretary firmly back in the company headquarters 'holding the fort'. If a manager and secretary communicated through an intercom between their offices in the 1960's who is to say in the 1990's that intercommunicator could not be miles apart instead of just yards?

INFORMATION TECHNOLOGY POLLUTES!

Most of the new technology is geared to bringing about the paperless environment. There is a view that managers spend most of their time in meetings and on the telephone.

With the onset of technology in office life, we not only store information in electronic or digital form, we also have a back-up of paper storage. Scores of offices duplicate all their filing electronically and in paper form. The huge metal filing cabinet has not gone away. The age of the paperless office is not yet with us. There is a marked resistance to a totally electronic environment. Having one's own files on disk does not solve the problems of what to do with every one else's paper that comes into the office. Technology is not yet up to what we want. We think we know what we want, technology has not yet made the step to provide us with what we need.

Technology is becoming cheaper all the time. By the year 2000 memory and processing power will be so cheap it will not be a limiting factor in the cost of information handling.

THE POSITIVE SIDE OF INFORMATION TECHNOLOGY

Information technology has enabled us to attain the following objectives;

1 **A reduction of information float:** (that is a decrease in the delay and uncertainty occasioned by the inaccessibility of information that is being typed, in the mail, has been misfiled, or is simply in an office that is closed for the weekend.)

2 **The elimination of redundant work:** (unnecessary tasks such as retyping and laborious manual filing and retrieval.)

3 **The better utilisation of human resources:** (for tasks that require judgement, initiative, and the human consideration touch.)

SUMMARY

- Information technology is good for secretarial and administrative staff as it frees up their time and helps them to be more efficient and effective at their jobs.

- Information technology does not eliminate paper, it merely reduces it.

HEALTH AND SAFETY

INTRODUCTION

A clean and safe working environment is of great benefit to both employers and employees alike. It demonstrates a commitment to the safety and well being of staff and in turn engenders a sense of worth and commitment from employees.

Employers are obliged by law to ensure a reasonable standard of health and safety at work. Employees, too, have a duty to take reasonable care of both themselves and those around them. Improved standards of health and safety have spin-offs in terms of better employee relationships, lower absenteeism and increased efficiency, better public image and bottom-line profitability. Is it no accident that employees who are most safety conscious work for firms with good accident records. It is also no accident that the firms with the best safety records in the United Kingdom are often numbered amongst the most profitable.

This chapter sets out to highlight your current responsibilities under existing legislation and how best those responsibilities can be utilised to provide a safe and healthy working environment for yourself and your colleagues.

THE HEALTH AND SAFETY AT WORK ACT 1974

Irrespective of who you are or what you do in an organisation the Health and Safety at Work Act applies to *you*. It covers everyone at work, whether you are employed or self employed. The 'Act' even provides protection for members of the public whose health and safety may be at risk as a result of your work activities. The Act recognises that employees, as well as employers have duties toward ensuring high standards of health and safety. But firstly let us consider the duties of the organisation you work for.

GENERAL DUTIES OF EMPLOYERS

WHAT SHOULD YOUR ORGANISATION BE PROVIDING FOR YOU?

The Act imposes a duty on every employer to ensure, so far as is reasonably practicable, the health, the safety and welfare at work of their employees. These general duties include that the following are to be safe and without risk to health so far as is reasonably practicable;

- plant and systems of work
  (machines, equipment and how the work is carried out)

- use, handling, storage, transport of articles and substances

- place of work, access to and egress from it (entrances, exits, gangways, corridors)

- working environment and adequate welfare facilities (clean, fresh air, first aid arrangements, drinking water)

These four areas as a whole should incorporate every work activity you are involved in whilst with the organisation. The general duty under the Act is therefore implying that whatever work activity you are involved in, your organisation must make sure you are doing it safely and without risk to your health, your colleagues' health or anybody else who may be affected by the activities you are involved in (i.e. the public).

The Act continues by saying that all employers must provide for you adequate information, instruction, training and supervision to enable safe working. The employer must ensure that new and existing employees receive the necessary health and safety information to do their job safely.

The most effective way of achieving this is to have a formal induction procedure where new employees can be given health and safety information relevant to their jobs *before* they are set to work. A brief mention of health and safety during an induction programme however is not sufficient. Regular training must also be provided to ensure staff remain familiar with health and safety procedures and learn about new policies and procedures relevant to their job.

The two categories of employee most likely at risk from health and safety hazards are either

(a) new employees – staff who are unaware of the hazards, risk implication of doing a job for the first time or

(b) long term staff – staff who have been with the organisation some considerable length of time who may have forgotten some health and safety procedures or simply become too familiar with a job causing them to cut corners, and become blasé.

This therefore highlights the need to induct, to train and then to retrain. The newer or inexperienced the employee, the greater the risks in the job, therefore the more training and supervision should be required.

Poster campaigns and safety notices should also be used to raise and maintain awareness in health and safety issues together with a good health and safety policy.

SO FAR AS IS REASONABLY PRACTICABLE

Time and time again you will see the phrase 'So far as is reasonably practicable'. Your organisation must provide a safe place of work so far as is reasonably practicable. But what does this actually mean? This is a key phrase in the Act.

This means the organisation must weigh up the costs of providing a safe system of work against the risk to health and safety (if one did not provide the safe system). Only if the costs are grossly disproportionate to the risks can the safety precaution not be considered to be 'reasonably practicable solutions. For example the 'cost' of keeping walkways and fire exits clear is not disproportionately high when compared with the risk to safety.

SAFETY POLICIES

Any organisation which employs five people or more must have a health and safety policy statement. The policy is an illustration of your organisation's commitment to health and safety and should highlight how the management team in the organisation intend to provide a safe working environment for all employees. The policy must be signed and dated by the most senior person responsible for health and safety in the organisation and updated every two to three years to coincide with changes in policy and personnel.

The health and safety policy must be brought to the attention of all employees at the earliest possible time. Many organisations make the mistake of simply pinning the safety policy on the board in the hope that employees will stop and read it. However how many times do you walk past a notice board and never ever bother to read what is there. Evidence suggests that less than 10% of what is displayed on a notice board is actually read and understood. The most effective way to communicate the contents of the health and safety policy to ensure employees understand what is expected of them is by induction and training – face to face communication.

- Always ask to see your health and safety policy so you are clear as to your responsibilities and how best to achieve those.

GENERAL DUTIES OF EMPLOYEES

What should you be doing for your organisation?

The Health and Safety at Work Act also recognises the importance of employee involvement in providing a safe working environment for you and imposes the following duties:

Every employee has a duty;

- 'To take reasonable care for the health and safety of themselves and of others who may be affected by your ACTS or OMISSIONS at work'.

By Acts and Omissions it means not only the things you do in the workplace but also the things you fail to do both of which can result in you or a colleague having our accident.

- 'To co-operate with your employer so far as it is necessary to enable them to fulfil their legal obligations'

This statement firmly suggests that all employees must read and comply with current safety policies, follow safer systems of work, take part in fire drills, report all health and safety hazards to the relevant personnel.

- 'The final duty involving employees states that no person shall intentionally or recklessly interfere with or misuse anything provided in the interests of health, safety or welfare'.

The most common example of employees not complying with the above duty are:

- putting pieces of wood underneath fire doors to keep them ajar when clearly fire doors should be kept closed at all times.

- defacing or removing safety notices.

- removing fire extinguishers from walls and using them as 'door stops'.

All employees must accept that they too have responsibilities under the Health and Safety at Work Act, a breach of which can lead to individuals being prosecuted.

SAFETY CHECKLIST FOR EMPLOYEES

- Read and understand your organisation's health and safety policy.

- Be clear about your health and safety responsibilities.

- Know your nearest fire exit.

- Know where your assembly point is

- Would you know which extinguisher to use on what fire?

- Would you know how to use the relevant extinguisher?

- Can all your employees hear the fire alarm? (noisy environments/hard of hearing).

- Are your fire routes/exits unlocked and free from obstruction?

- Where is your nearest First Aider?

- Always ask to attend your organisation's induction programme.

- Have you received relevant health and safety training prior to being set to work?

- Are you familiar with your organisations Accident Reporting procedure?

- If you have an accident who do you report this to?

- Who is responsible for the accident book?

FIRE SAFETY

Fire in Britain causes the death of approximately 1000 people every year. Many of these deaths occur in the workplace and are clearly preventable.

Fires occur in the majority of cases because of people's failure to know their organisations fire procedures and to follow them.

Every employee should know the actions they need to take in the event of fire and how to evacuate the premises quickly and safely. This section offers you a guide in fire safety.

Circumstances will determine the exact procedure appropriate for your organisation, but every employee should receive adequate training and instructions and fully understand them. In the event of a fire breaking out it should be possible to take prompt and effective action along the following lines:

1 Raising the alarm

2 Immediate action attack

3 Evacuation

1 Sound the fire alarm from the nearest available call point. Always familiarise yourself with the call points particularly those in your immediate work area.

2 Where there is no *immediate danger to life* warn people within the vicinity by shouting FIRE, calling for help to fight the fire with the appropriate fire extinguisher.

- Always fight the fire standing between the fire and the fire exit – do not cut off your fire exit.

  If you are unable to extinguish the fire or consider it too dangerous to continue then immediately RAISE THE ALARM closing all doors/windows, to prevent the spread of the fire, on leaving the room.

FIRE EXTINGUISHER CHART

CLASS OF FIRE	TYPE OF EXTINGUISHER			
	WATER (RED)	SPRAYFOAM (GREEN)	CO_2 GAS (BLACK)	POWDER (BLUE)
A paper, wood, textile &fabric	✓	✓		✓
B flammable liquids		✓	✓	✓
C flammable gases			✓	✓
electrical hazard			✓	✓
vehicle protection		✓		✓

3 *Evacuation*

The fire alarm should always be taken as a signal to leave the building and should be understood by you and your colleagues.

Leave your work area immediately closing all doors and windows behind you but do not stop or return to pick up personal belongings.

TIME MEANS LIVES

Leave by your nearest fire exit. If this is blocked use your alternative fire route making your way to the assembly point for a roll call.

NEVER USE A LIFT DURING A FIRE

- Know your fire procedures.

- Know your nearest fire exit.

- Always attend fire drills – it could save your life!

- Use fire safety checklist.

VDU'S

On 1 January 1993, a law came into force entitled the Display Screen Equipment Regulations (DSE). This means that all employers who employ staff and use VDUs on a regular basis must carry out what is known as a VDU assessment. These assessments are an opportunity for employers to consider whether their employees are using VDUs safely, and in so doing limit the adverse effects that may occur during regular but improper use, eg eye, neck and backache, painful wrists and fingers.

Increasingly the job of carrying out assessments on VDU workstations is becoming the responibility of the administrator. Below is a step by step guide to many of the points you need to consider during an assessment. If you have any doubts always refer back to your organisation's safety policy on VDUs.

CHECKLIST FOR OPERATORS OF VDU EQUIPMENT

1 Users should be able to adopt a 'straight on' sitting position – no twists in the neck, trunk or legs.

Viewing distance should be 500-70cms from eye to screen

The users sightline to the top of the screen should be slightly below the horizontal to avoid fatigue in neck and muscles.

Users should be able to focus on objects far away frequently without altering their work position.

Users should experiment until they find the most comfortable position. If sitting at another workstation for any length of time this should be adjusted to be as comfortable as possible.

2 **Exercise at the workstation**
At work it is possible to relax tense muscles at your workstation.

Shoulders	Shrug upwards – hold a few seconds – relax – rotate 5 times forwards, 5 times backwards.
Neck	Gently nod forwards and backwards and side to side. Do not rotate the neck in a circle.
Arms	Stretch arms out straight – tense muscles and relax. 5 times.
Fingers	Clench into fists and then open out with fingers outstretched. 5 times. Relax hands and shake them.

Eyes Cup hands over open eyes for a few seconds, focus on a distant object for several seconds, blink rapidly for 5 and slowly for 5.

Take deep breaths between these exercises. Take a walk outside in your lunch break if the weather is fine. Make use of natural breaks – coffee time, moving to another office area etc, to stretch muscles.

3 **Screen Breaks**
Try and take a break from screen based duties of 10 minutes within any one hour to avoid the onset of fatigue, eg telephone calls, opening mail.

4 **Cleaning**
The screen must be cleaned by operators once a week using only the cleaning materials available from your line manager.

5 **Reflection and glare**
Check reflection and glare and cleanliness of screen and anti-glare screen.

Windows may produce reflections on screens or give a 'washed out' image due to lack of contrast. This results in viewing difficulty. Try to avoid the screens facing windows directly eg, with operators back to the window. It is best to position the VDU at a right angle to the window. If this is not possible e.g. with adjacent window walls, then window blinds, screens or filters may be useful. White or reflective surfaces should be avoided as much as possible in the area of the VDU.

6 **Health**
Discuss any concerns regarding working with the VDU with your line manager.

VDU ASSESSMENT

Use this checklist (in conjunction with the user of the VDU equipment) to identify possible risks to the user arising from the use of the equipment.

Office Location _____   Name of Assessor _____

VDU Identity _____   Date of Assessment _____

Name of User _____
(or person present at assessment)

HEALTH

Time spent on display screen

HEALTH

Do you experience any general health problems working with VDUs?	YES / NO	Describe
Do you have any specific aches and pains working on VDU equipment?	YES / NO	Describe
Do you experience any eyesight difficulties when using VDU equipment?	YES / NO	Describe

NOTE:
If at any time the user does experience any of the above conditions as a result of working on the VDU equipment, he/she must report it to their supervisor.

KEY ACTIONS FOR ADMINISTRATORS

- Read your organisation's health and safety policy.

   Ensure you are fully aware of your health and safety responsibilities whilst at work.

- Locate your nearest fire exit.

- Find out where your assembly point is situated. Familiarise yourself with relevant fire extinguishers.

- If you have an accident at work – are you clear who this should be reported to?

- Find out who is your nearest First Aider.

- Are you aware of who your safety representative is?

- Ensure you receive awareness training on the correct/best use of equipment whilst working at a VDU.

- Ensure you have been trained in the health and safety aspects before you operate potentially hazardous equipment.

  – photocopier

  – shredder

  – cleaning fluids

- Keep all gangways clear and free of obstruction.

Remember: Health and safety is *not* somebody else's problem – it is *yours*!

SETTING UP MEETINGS, CONFERENCES AND EXHIBITIONS

- Shaping and planning
- Budgeting
- Choosing the venue
- Running it on the day
- Stage managing a conference
- Organising and designing an exhibition stand

SHAPING AND PLANNING

What should you do when your boss asks you to arrange a meeting? Time spent on finding out this information in the beginning can save you valuable time, effort and money later, particularly if you are using external facilities. First ask your boss the following questions.

When should it be arranged for?

Where should it be held?

Why is it being held?

Who is it being held for?

What time should it start?

Will refreshments/lunch be required?

Any special requirements?

The answers to these questions will form the basis of your plan. However, all the details may not be finalised, but do start to make a rough plan e.g. 'Sales team meeting to discuss targets. Company training room. Morning only. Maximum 10 people'.

If this is a regular meeting look at any previous files to see what has been organised in the past. Find out how successful they were and if there were any problems. Use the information as a guide and then make your plan using this knowledge. A lot can be learnt from past mistakes.

CHECKLIST

Summarise the main information and create a 'checklist' and record the date each item is actioned. When you are busy it is easy to forget and this will remind you of anything that has not yet been arranged. Keep it simple and update it straight away. The following guide can be altered to suit your needs. Keep this attached to your file for easy reference.

SUMMARY AND CHECKLIST

Meeting
Date(s)
Venue
Room name/no.
Number attending
Timings
Room set up

	Date	Contact name & tel no.
Accommodation		
Audio Visual Aids		
Catering		
Display		
Invitation letter		
Literature		
Location Map		
Transport		
Venue/Meeting Room		

MEETING ROOM

Check that a suitable venue/meeting room is available on this date. If it is make a provisional booking immediately to ensure you have a room. If you are using an external venue read the section on 'venues'.

WHO CAN ATTEND

If the date has not already been discussed, ring each person or their secretary to check they can attend and ask them to pencil the date in their diary.

INVITATION

Inform everyone officially of Where, When, Why the meeting is taking place. If you are using an unfamiliar venue a location map should be sent, so everyone will know how to get there. (See section on Stage Managing a Conference for more detail on location maps).

ROOM SET UP

The room should be set up in a 'style' suitable for the meeting. Most small meetings generally require everyone to sit around one table, boardroom style. There are four main set up styles and the following diagram should help when discussing this with any conference manager.

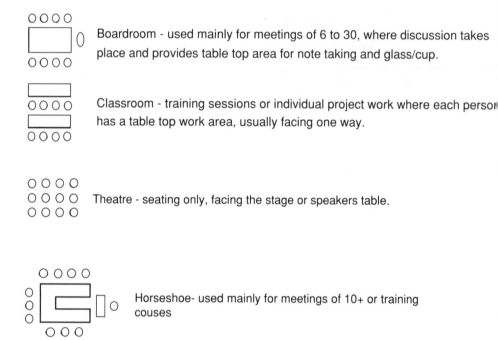

Boardroom - used mainly for meetings of 6 to 30, where discussion takes place and provides table top area for note taking and glass/cup.

Classroom - training sessions or individual project work where each person has a table top work area, usually facing one way.

Theatre - seating only, facing the stage or speakers table.

Horseshoe- used mainly for meetings of 10+ or training couses

CATERING

Make arrangements for any refreshments ie. coffee on arrival or throughout the meeting. Water and/or squash during the meeting. Lunch or other requirements should be discussed and agreed with the catering or conference manager before the meeting. They will require 'final numbers' (usually) 48 hours in advance. Do check.

AUDIO VISUAL

A flip chart and pens may be all that is needed and most venues and meeting rooms will have these. Do check that pens work and there is enough paper left. If other equipment is required see the section on Stage Managing a Conference.

CHOOSING THE VENUE

Choosing the right venue is essential and will ensure a successful meeting/conference. During the planning stage you made certain key decisions – location, date(s), numbers, and established what facilities you need. Now to finding the venue that meets all of these. Every meeting/conference has its own special requirements, so first look at the main requirements, location, size of room(s), catering facilities, standard. You may have a long list of venues that all appear suitable, so look at the less essential but advantageous details such as leisure facilities, large car park etc. To assist you with selecting the right venue you may find the following of help.

YELLOW PAGES

Useful for local venues

THE CONFERENCE BLUE AND GREEN BOOKS

List a large number of venues which are broken down into areas and have detailed descriptions, photographs and general information. Do check you have the latest edition.

VENUE FINDING AGENCIES

The 'professionals' will make a shortlist of venues that meet your requirements. This can save you a lot of time and many are able to negotiate a better deal than you could by booking the venue direct. Do ask them to check essential details before you visit so that your time is not wasted.

CONVENTION BUREAU/TOURIST BOARDS

Will make helpful suggestions and give you telephone numbers to contact and or send you brochures.

HOTEL GROUPS CENTRAL RESERVATIONS FOR MEETINGS/CONFERENCES

Should you need to book a number of venues around the country for a series of meetings you may find keeping to one hotel group is the answer.

Once you have made your selection, make a short list of suitable venues. Telephone the Conference Manager at each venue, double check the details just in case there was a printing error and find out if the venue is available on the date you want. They may not all be available; if the venue *is* available, ask them to provisionally reserve it for you. If you do not you may find that when you ring back a week later the venue may now be provisionally booked by another company. Do not forget to check the availability of

ALL your requirements. Do ask about other bookings they have on the same day – your manager may not be too happy if the 18-30 Club have booked the venue for a Summer '93 reunion!

Ask the Conference Manager to confirm the provisional booking(s) and costs in writing and arrange a convenient date to visit the venue. Allow plenty of time – do not hurry the visit, see as much as possible and get a feel for the venue and write down your own comments about the venue and staff. If you are visiting 2, 3 or 4 venues in one day it is essential that you write down your comments on each as by the end of the day you will find it difficult to remember everything!

DO	**DON'T**
Make a shortlist	Be persuaded not to visit
Check information given	Forget your checklist
Make a provisional booking	Leave it too late
Give written confirmation	Assume anything
Visit the venue	Make a quick decision
Take time to see everything	Rely on verbal agreements
Ask advice from venue manager	Panic
Ask advice from Bureau/ Agency	
Taste the food	
Say that you are considering other venues	
Get references	
Make notes on your visit	

VISITING A VENUE – WHAT TO LOOK FOR

- Accommodation – standard and size of rooms

- Air conditioning in meeting room (if the room is too hot the delegates may fall asleep. If it is too cold they won't be able to concentrate)

- Additional facilities available – leisure complex, close to town centre

- Availability

- Audio visual equipment – complimentary/for hire

- Car park – do delegates have to pay and how much?

- Catering – quality and service

- Cloakroom – where is it located?

- Delegate rate (what's included?)

- Height of ceiling in meeting room – will projection screen fit?

- Location and ease of access for delegates

- Maximum/minimum number delegates in meeting room

- Natural daylight in meeting room

- Notice Board

- Office available for conference organiser

- Refreshments during the meeting, where will they be?

- Registration Desk(s) – what type of covering is available?

- Staff – are they helpful and polite?

- Standard of venue – professional, clean?

- Technician for audio visual equipment – provided complimentary/cost

- Toilet facilities – distance from the meeting room/clean?

- Transport to station/town centre, what is available?

- VIP suite – standard/size?

BUDGETING

One of the main factors you will need to know is The Budget. If you have not been given a budget, ask. The company's annual budget could be spent on one event. With the budget agreed you can start to plan, Gleneagles may meet all your requirements, but if you only have a small budget you will be wasting a lot of time and possibly money. It is impossible to keep within an unknown budget, however, once it is agreed, keep to it. You may find that the requirements alter slightly, if this happens be aware that this could affect the final cost. Wild and wonderful ideas sound great and can create impact, but so can the cost. Always get agreement from your manager before confirming any additional expenditure.

Prepare a budget sheet, listing ALL items of expenditure and costs. This will help you keep to the agreed budget and help when you submit your report after the event. Don't forget any extras!

VENUE CHARGES

Venues vary in how they cost meeting/conference rooms. The two main methods are:

1 Items charged separately according to requirements
Room Hire
Coffee/Biscuits

Lunch
Dinner
Accommodation
Audio Visual
Refreshments

Do ask what time you can set up from, as you may need extra time for the technician to set up and check the audio visual equipment. It is just as important to know what time you have the room until. They may have booked another company in for an evening meeting or dinner. However, if the room is not in use the evening, or even the day before, they may let up you set up early at no extra charge – but don't count on it. Allow time to dismantle and remove audio visual equipment. A surcharge may be added to the bill if the room is not cleared by the agreed time or, they may turn all the lights out and power off.

2 Delegate Rate – Day and 24 hour rate

Day Rate (8 Hours)
Room hire
Coffee/Biscuits
Luncheon
Tea/Biscuits

24 Hour Rate
Room hire
Coffee/Biscuits
Luncheon
Tea/Biscuits
Accommodation
Dinner
Breakfast

IMPORTANT ITEMS TO BE CONSIDERED

CATERING

- Coffee/biscuits on arrival are not always included in the delegate rate.

- Refreshments during lunch are not always included in the delegate rate.

- When ordering wine it is advisable to state the number of bottles of white and red to be on each table. Otherwise you may have a larger than expected bill.

- Ask for the menus applicable to the Delegate Rate. Often this is hot/cold buffet. If the menu is not suitable discuss this with the catering manager. The venue will ask you to confirm the number of delegates for catering purposes at least 48 hours in advance, some may require final numbers earlier. Remember that this is the number you will be charged for, regardless of the actual number.

ACCOMMODATION

- Do ask to look at the bedrooms on your visit.

- What is the standard of bedroom? Twin bedded, double, single, executive?

- Do they all have ensuite bathrooms with shower?

- Is the 24 hour delegate rate for single or twin occupancy?

- What time can delegates have their rooms from?

- What time must the rooms be vacated on departure?

- Is breakfast English or continental? There may be a supplement for English.

ROOM HIRE – WHAT IS INCLUDED

Table, chairs, pens, pads, water/cordial/mints, flip charts, screen, overhead and carousel projector, video PA system, microphones. You may find you can save a lot of time and money if these items are included in the delegate rate, provided by the venue.

QUOTATIONS

When you book the venue or order any additional items make sure they confirm the prices. Do check that the prices are the same as the original quotation. Mistakes do happen or they may have increased their prices.

DISCOUNTS

You may be able to negotiate a discount, depending on the time of year, expected availability, the venue's main business (corporate, individuals or groups) and their sales and marketing policies. If you have booked through a Venue Finding Company they receive commission direct from the venue, so generally you don't pay for their services. They may be able to offer you a better rate than if you book direct.

INVOICES

Invoices should be sent to your company for your attention. Most venues will ask for a deposit prior to the event, some require payment in full prior to the event and others will invoice you after. Do get confirmation on this and a copy of terms and conditions of hire.

If your company has an account with a business travel agency they may be able to book the venue for you and have the invoices sent direct to them.

STAGE MANAGING A CONFERENCE

In simple terms – how to organise all the practical arrangements. Organising a conference is not so different to organising a meeting, but generally there are many more additional arrangements to be made needing careful planning.

Conferences are an excellent method of bringing people together to discuss areas of interest, whether on a professional or personal basis, however, give some thought to the following:

- WHY is the conference taking place?

- What do you expect to achieve?

- Who should be there?

- Are the speakers professional and interesting?

- Has the best venue been selected for the purpose of this conference?

- How long is each presentation?

So before you go any further, gather together all the information you have and make a list leaving plenty of space to make notes. Many of the following were covered in the shaping and planning section, however larger conferences may require additional arrangements to be organised before the day.

- Venue name and address
- Conference Manager – name and telephone number
- Name of Conference Room(s)
- Number of Delegates Attending
- Accommodation
- Audio Visual Equipment
- Badges
- Chairperson
- Conference Room Set Up
- Catering
- Display/Graphics
- List of Delegates
- List of Speakers
- Literature
- Location Map
- Stage Set
- Timetable of the conference
- Top Table for Speakers and Chairperson
- Transport
- Venue

AUDIO VISUAL EQUIPMENT

The equipment you use will depend on the requirements of the speakers and the sophistication of the conference. The equipment mainly used and available to hire is:

- Slide Projector (Carousel)

- Overhead Projector

- Video

- Screen

- Flip charts

- Pointer

Should you require more professional usage, higher quality technical equipment is available and you should consult a specialist.

Images can be projected from in front of the screen and the equipment is positioned in the middle or at the back of the audience. However, back projection where the equipment is approximately 10' behind the screen, out of view, is a more professional method. You must allow for the additional space required for this. The height of the screen is very important and make sure that all delegates will be able to see clearly. Check that the ceiling is high enough.

PA systems are permanent fixtures in the larger venues. If your chosen venue does not have this facility you can hire them. Using a PA system will create a professional atmosphere and ensure that all delegates can hear. Decide how many microphones and what type you will need, or if you are using a production company they can advise you. The main types of microphone/supports are:

- Stand – full height adjustable with cable

microphone, can be hand held

- Table Top – cable microphone

- Clip/Lapel – small microphone that is clipped to speakers clothing

- Roving/Radio – no cable giving freedom for speaker to move around

BADGES

These should be printed before the conference and inserted into badge holders. Badge printing machines are available. Using different colour badges denoting – delegate, speaker etc. can help identification. Name badges are very useful when delegates do not know each other. It is also a good idea for safety and security purposes. These should be given to delegates on arrival. Laying the badges out in alphabetical order neatly will make it easier for registration staff to give out the correct badge quickly.

CHAIRPERSON

The chairperson is the key person at the event and will hold the conference together ensuring that the conference keeps to the planned timetable.

LITERATURE

It is likely that you will need to produce several items of literature for the conference. This will need to be arranged in advance especially if it has to be designed and printed. Do ask for this to be delivered before the event, just in case there have been any mistakes, as it will be too late on the day to re-print. The literature required will vary depending on the needs of the conference.

LOCATION MAP

Delegates will need to know where the conference is being held and how to find it. A good location map should show the surrounding area, road numbers of main routes, names of local roads, landmarks, stations, airports and how long it takes to get there approximately. It should be clear and simple and sent to all delegates, speakers and any other guests, contractors etc. This can be printed as part of the conference brochure or on the back of the invitation. These are often provided by the venue or can be copied from their brochure.

CATERING

Catering should be provided for delegates and if the conference is an all day event lunch or lunch facilities should be made available. If the delegates have not had lunch or the food is unsatisfactory it is unlikely that the delegates will be able to concentrate during the afternoon session. If the food is poor that may be the most memorable part of the conference. Do check the standard of food at the venue as often this is overlooked.

REGISTRATION

An area close to the entrance of the conference room should be set aside for registering delegates. Badges should

be given out to delegates on arrival or print out a list of delegates and tick them as they arrive. This may be useful after the conference to see who did not attend.
Registration staff should be briefed before the event on the facilities available and the conference timetable/speakers etc. They must be able to answer any questions that delegates may ask, or know where they can get further help.

REHEARSAL

Will the speakers and the production/technical team need a rehearsal? It may be possible to do a run through before the conference starts, but if there are a number of speakers and a complex light show, music, slides, video presentation then the conference room should be booked for the day before for set up and rehearsal. Often there will be a reduction on the daily room hire charge for this, do check as this will be an extra cost to come out of your budget.

ROOM SET UP

Setting up the room Theatre style will allow you to seat the maximum number of delegates. A central aisle and two side aisles will give delegates easy access, however, this will depend on safety regulations at the venue. Discuss this with the conference manager. In addition you may wish to have question and answer sessions involving the audience. Stand microphones should be positioned in the aisles or you may prefer to use roving microphones passed to delegates by staff.

Will the delegates all remain in one conference room throughout the day(s)? Or do certain sessions require more discussion – perhaps breaking into smaller groups? If you decide to have break out sessions additional conference rooms will be required close by.

SPEAKERS

The choice of speakers is very important. How many speakers will be taking part at any one time? From this you can work out the number for the top table plus the chairperson. Will any of the speakers require special facilities? A disabled speaker may not be able to get on stage without assistance. A ramp may help. Many speakers charge for their services and for their expenses.

STAFF

Before the delegates arrive brief your staff on the main details giving them each a copy of the timetable, list of speakers, chairman. Give them the opportunity to ask any questions. Do make clear each person's responsibility and what it expected of them. Staff should not be allowed to smoke, drink, or eat in view of the delegates. Arrange for a room or area where they can go for their breaks and arrange with the Catering Manager for refreshments and lunch. If you are using a production company the crew will also need feeding so decide if you will pay for this. Make an allowance for the extra meals in your budget and final numbers.

STAGE SET

Depending on the nature of the conference, the image that your company wants to achieve and the budget, there are a number of things you can do. Contract a professional production company to design and produce a stage set, this can be anything from a few graphic panels with the company name and logo, a theme or a series of panels that tell 'a story'. You may also require lighting and music to help create atmosphere. One major company director likes to make his entrance with the theme from ROCKY.

TIMETABLE

The length of time given to each presentation should be no longer than 1 and a half hours to 2 hours without a break. Allow approximately half an hour for coffee/tea breaks if possible, as delegates may also need to contact their office. Remember that most people have a limited boredom threshold and will start to get restless unless there are enough 'attention grabbers'. This is where music and visual stimulation can play an exciting part. Even a change of voice tone, a question to the audience, or a joke can keep the conference alive.

TOP TABLE

This will be required for the speakers and chairperson, usually situated on a raised stage. Water/cordial, glasses, paper and pens should be provided. A lectern may be used for a speaker to stand behind and rest his or her papers. Microphones should be positioned to enable speakers/chairperson to make a professional presentation with ease.

TRANSPORT

Think about how delegates will arrive. If a large number will travel by car, check that the car park is large enough.

If it is an international conference many may travel by plane and/or train so check access. It may be that you need to hire a coach to transport staff. Make the arrangements with a reliable company and check there will be enough space for the coach in the car park.

RUNNING IT ON THE DAY

If possible book in to the hotel the night before, so that you feel fresh and ready for the day or 'daze' to come! Get up early, have a light breakfast – and don't try to do everything yourself – delegate. Meet with the person who has been appointed by the venue as your 'contact', walk around with them and use your checklist to see that everything you asked for has been organised. It's often the little items that get forgotten – pens, paper, water, glasses for the top table.

Delegate specific tasks to colleagues – check all the lights are working in the meeting rooms. One common problem is The Notice Board and the mis-spelling of your company name. The first person to see it is usually someone important! Not a good start to the day.

No mater how organised you are unless you have co-operation from the venue team it will seem like a very long day. Ask their advice and help, after all they do this every day, get them on your side.

Do find time to relax and enjoy the event and if you can, sit and listen to the speakers, it is always useful to see the meeting/conference from the delegates point of view. Make notes for ideas on how to improve things next time. There is always room for improvement and remember that you are probably the most critical person there. Minor problems tend to go unnoticed and as long as bigger problems are sorted out quickly, apologise for any inconvenience and with a smile – this will not spoil the day. Keep people informed of any changes, don't assume they know.

Although at the end of the day(s) you may feel exhausted, organising a meeting/conference can give a tremendous feeling of personal achievement.

Do check the following.

- Audio Visual Equipment

- Depending on the sophistication of the meeting and the requirements of the speakers you may require a technician. Check with the technician that all the slides etc. from the speakers are ready and in order and that everyone has a timetable of who is on and when.

If you do not need a technician ensure that the equipment is working, correctly positioned and that spare bulbs (light bulbs), carousels, flip chart pads etc. are available should they be needed.

REGISTRATION

For meetings where delegates do not know each other it is useful to give everyone a badge. Arrange to have a desk to lay out the badges neatly in alphabetical order, this will help you and your colleagues to find them quickly and tick the delegates name on the list of attendees. Registration staff should know where the 'facilities' are, cloakroom, toilets, public telephones, coffee area to assist delegates.

CATERING

Check throughout the day that the catering team are ready

before each break just in case the meeting finishes earlier than planned. Watch that they do not make a lot of noise during the meeting as this will be distracting for the delegates. Do eat the food etc. so you can be sure that the quality is good.

ORGANISING AND DESIGNING AN EXHIBITION STAND

The main points to consider are:

1 Stand Objectives

2 Budget

3 Stand Booking

4 Stand Design

5 Exhibitors Manual/Guide

6 Stand Manager

7 Stand Staffing and Training

REMEMBER – CHECK EVERYTHING, NEVER ASSUME ANYTHING

Recently one week before I was due to build a stand in a Bristol hotel, I rang to check the time for setting up the exhibition. I was told that the exhibition was NOT being held there, so I immediately rang the organisers – they had changed the venue! A phone call before the exhibition will save you the time and trouble on the day.

STAND OBJECTIVES

What do you expect to achieve from the exhibition?

Think carefully about WHY you are exhibiting as this will be a key factor in planning your stand. Is your marketing campaign targeted at a specific market? Is this the right exhibition for your service or product?

REASONS TO EXHIBIT

Increase Sales?

Brand Awareness?

PR purposes?

Meet new clients?

Hospitality for existing clients?

Launch New Product?

See what your competitors are doing?

Carry out testing or research?

BUDGET

This should include the following:

Shell Scheme Package or Space cost

Design and Construction (if applicable)

Furniture

Power and Lighting

Preparation and Transport of exhibits

Graphics and display items

Literature, sales lead pads, pens

Stand catering/entertaining

Personnel – transport, hotels, expenses, parking

Promotional staff

Promotional clothing, gifts

Audio visual equipment

Always ask for written quotations and check these against the invoices, mistakes can happen.

STAND BOOKING

Request the following information about the exhibition. If you are responsible for booking the stand you will need to know what budget is available and the cost to exhibit. If the stand is already booked check the information sent by the organisers.

SALES BROCHURE

This will help you understand who the visitors will be, the dates of the exhibition, the venue, the costs, the marketing campaign, name and telephone number of the organisers and PR manager.

FLOOR PLAN

When booking a stand or if it has already been booked and confirmed, check the stand number and size. The size of stand you need will depend on your objectives, budget, number of sales/technical staff, size or number of products and image. Your stand may have a pillar or other intrusion shown, check this with the organisers as it may cause you problems later if you are not aware of it.

STAND PACKAGES

There are 2 main stand packages available Shell Scheme

and Space Only. These will vary slightly depending on the package offered by the organisers. If the information in the brochure is unclear, find out exactly what is included.

A) SHELL SCHEME PACKAGE

A modular system consisting of side and back wall panels, either melamine coated or fabric covered. Each panel is usually 1m wide and 2.5m high and joined together by upright supports of metal or wood. Graphics or posters can be attached to the panels using the correct fixing, either Velcro or sticky pads.

Fascia or name panel and stand number. This will help visitors find your stand. Each stand is numbered and marked on the floor plan within the exhibition and/or in the show catalogue.

Carpet or floor covering. The colour will vary so ask the organisers what will be on your stand and what will be in the aisles.

ELECTRICS

Some power points or lighting may be included. The organisers will appoint an official contractor. Information and forms will be included in the exhibitors manual.

FURNITURE

Often not included. The organisers can recommend a supplier or may appoint an official contractor. Information and forms will be included in the exhibitors' manual.

B) SPACE ONLY

As it sounds, you get Floor Space only. You may decide

that this is the best option when you intend to have a stand designed and built, have an existing stand (often designed to be used at several exhibitions) or purchase a modular exhibition stand system. Find out where your company intends to use these and be aware of any potential problems if you have an existing stand. Watch out for the following:

Height restrictions

Systems too small/large

Worn out

STAND DESIGN

This can be quite simple, just one or two graphic panels or posters, literature and/or your product. Alternatively you may need the professional help of a stand designer/contractor to design and build a stand.

Discuss this carefully with your colleagues/boss and before you arrange a meeting with prospective stand designers write a DESIGN BRIEF. This should give the following information, applicable to your stand, clearly and simply.

Name of Exhibition

Dates for build up and breakdown

Venue/Location

Stand Objectives

Budget – specify what this should include – design, production, construction, transport, dismantling, electric's, furniture, graphics, carpet, audio visual etc.

Dimensions and floor plan

Services (water and waste for sink unit if you want a kitchen)

Products/Service – what products, quantity, size

Corporate colours or logo

Image you want to promote – product/service/company

Special Feature – new product?

Competition – and briefly how this will be organised

Promotional campaign linked with exhibition

Audio Visual – ie: promotional video to be shown every hour

Ask colleagues if they can recommend any or contact the exhibition organiser. Do ask for and check references if you have not used the designer/contractor before. When the brief has been agreed, ring and invite each to a meeting, give them literature on your products/services that will help them to design your stand. They may have alternative suggestions that could be of benefit to you, so take notes. Ask each to submit a design proposal and written quotation. Ensure that the chosen design meets your brief and that both you and the designer/contractor are happy with it. Always inform your chosen designer of ANY changes immediately, as delay could lead to endless expense.

The designer/contractor will build your stand on the dates allocated by the organisers for space only build. You will need to liaise with them regarding the day and time you can deliver your products and literature ready for the opening of the exhibition.

At the end of the exhibition they will dismantle the stand. If you agreed to re-use the stand at another show they will then store it until required.

Do NOT leave the stand unattended at the end of the show, especially if you have valuable items or anything you need to keep.

GRAPHICS

These are photographs or images depicting your products or services and should be produced by a professional graphic company. If you are using a stand designer they can arrange for these to be produced as part of the stand brief. There are a variety of formats – pictures, graphs or information and should be in a uniform style. Make sure that the graphics are up-to-date and in good condition. Remember these reflect your company's image. Do not try to fill all the wall space as this will create an untidy and unattractive display. Graphics should be mounted on a material that is light weight, but durable and can be fixed to the wall panels either with velcro or sticky pads. Keep it simple, but attractive.

EXHIBITORS MANUAL/GUIDE/ACTION FILE

Most organisers will provide you with a comprehensive Exhibitor Manual/Guide or Action File that contains detailed information relating to that exhibition. Do read it, use the checklists and forms provided. There will be deadlines for you to return many of the forms by, so complete and return them in time. Some are easy to use and others look like the continuing saga of War and Peace. If you don't understand anything, ASK the organisers. Most are helpful and used to dealing with questions from new exhibitors as well as those that have exhibited many times before.

STAND MANAGER

This may be you. Ensure everyone is aware of who is appointed from the start. Also appoint an assistant, so that no matter what happens there is someone else who knows what has been actioned and can take over, if necessary. Remember it is not an easy task to take over if you have not been involved from the early stages so make sure the checklist is up-to-date, keep copies of orders and notes from meetings. If you think something has not been actioned – CHECK.

Look at your stand objectives, decide how and who can best achieve these. Once you have made the decision ensure that all personnel involved are briefed on what is expected of them – prior and during the exhibition. Delegate responsibilities and hold a stand briefing session to keep staff informed. Organise a daily rota including breaks. A training session on 'How to sell at an exhibition' could be beneficial.

Remember to take an emergency kit

>   –Sellotape
>
>   –Blue Tack
>
>   –Paper clips
>
>   –Scissors
>
>   –Enquiry Pads
>
>   –Envelopes
>
>   –Headed Paper
>
>   –Pens
>
>   –Velcro
>
>   –Sticky Pads

–String

–Stamps

–Tissues

–Polish and cloths

A lockable cupboard is very useful to keep personal belongings safe. Take only essential items with you.

A first aid kit is useful, however the venue should provide first aid.

PERSONNEL

Be selective when choosing your stand personnel. Think of these points:

–Image

–Knowledge of Product/Service

–Client Contact

–Technical Knowledge

–Communication – speech and body language

–Personality

–Company Knowledge

–Languages

A few hints for staff

ON THE STAND, DO NOT:

–Look bored or uninterested

-Smoke

-Ignore visitors because they didn't look like an MD

-Sit

-Form 'company' groups

-Eat or drink

-Jump on visitors

-Run down the competition

ON THE STAND, DO:

-Take regular breaks

-Look presentable

-Wear smart, but comfortable shoes

-Take a spare pair of shoes

-Be polite at all times

-Treat every visitor as a potential client

-Be relaxed

-Let your natural personality show

-Collect business cards

-Use enquiry pads or light pens

-Ensure you have plenty of business cards

-Keep all literature on display, restocked and tidy

-Follow up leads straight after the event

EXHIBITORS' RECEPTION

Some organisers arrange an exhibitors' reception during

the exhibition, which is a good opportunity for you to meet the organisers and other exhibitors in a relaxed environment. Exhibitions can be tiring, enjoyable and a great way to make new contacts, increase sales, meet your existing customers and more.

Remember those who visit the exhibition do so because they are interested enough to attend and want to know more about your product or service.

SUMMARY

- check everything never assume
- don't panic
- avoid making quick decisions
- listen to professional advice
- get written quotations
- delegate
- common sense
- use your checklists
- keep within budget
- be polite and helpful
- organise your time